Melange

and Other

I.T. Stories

Peter Hassebroek

Also by Peter Hassebroek

Upbound

Melange and Other I.T. Stories

Published by
Upbound Solutions, Ajax, Ontario, Canada

ISBN: 978-0-9866640-2-1

www.peterhassebroek.com

Contents

MELANGE

0001

By now all his colleagues in the IT department have settled at their desks.

Dustin Freeman enters through the revolving door of the weather-less office tower, brushes snow from his coat, and strolls to a bank of four elevators. There he waits with another man who deftly cradles a hot paper cup of tea while glancing at the recessed globes of glowing numbers. A rotund woman approaches. She struggles to balance two green shopping bags from the crooks of her elbows. A shiny teal-and-maroon DexiaTel badge, like the one in Dustin's pocket, dangles from a thin chain around her neck. Coatless and at ease, this pair, whom he's never seen before, regard Dustin as an intruder.

A sharp ting. Dustin pauses to let them on first but they change their minds. He shrugs, pleased to be alone again once the heavy doors slide closed. Dustin watches the tiny television screen above, ignoring the redness of the stock market numbers and focusing on the time: ten-thirteen. He's late but he's shown up later than this before. The doors open on the fifth-floor foyer where large panes of frosted glass bracket a massive mahogany door.

Dustin inserts his plastic badge in the slot to the right of the entrance, eyes fixed on the bead-sized bulb above. Red, red, red, he wills, as he pulls the card out. But no. The light displays a bright green, the door clicks. Dustin sighs with mock dejection as he pulls the handle.

A corridor of fading grey carpet inlaid with pastel-coloured geometric patterns circumnavigates the floor. The well-vacuumed laneway divides walled single-window offices from dozens of low-rise cubicles like a moat. Some of the office doors are open; most are not. Several have their blinds drawn. Limp Christmas decorations hang over a number of the cubicles, obscuring nameplates, workstation identifiers, and fading cartoon strips. People tap away at keyboards or speak on the phone; some entertain visitors who lean against the dusty blue risers. Sounds of busyness blending with the hum of white noise. No one pays Dustin any heed and he heeds no one. His anonymity, at one time unsettling, is now something he desires.

An intense discussion is underway in a small, cramped meeting room inside which more than a dozen people surround a narrow oval table. A few have rolled in chairs from cubicles. Their faces remain in his memory but many of the names are receding; somehow, that's reassuring. One person is talking to a complicated diagram of boxes, circles, diamonds, and arrows, black text on red, blue, green, and brown symbols spanning three panels of whiteboard. The rest appear confused or perhaps are distracted by the nearly empty donut carton, the wall, their BlackBerry devices; a fat woman appears to be dozing.

At last, Dustin reaches the double-cubicle cosily tucked away in a low traffic area in the southeast corner. His office. His sanctuary. His prison. His routine.

Turn computer on, take off coat, sit and spin twice, check for voice mail—"Your mailbox is empty"—and wait. And wait. And wait, as the computer processor chugs away, groaning and whirring, displaying images and scrolling text, flashing lights, red and green. What to do today, Dustin wonders, during the several minutes this takes. Between personal calls, bathroom visits, snack machine purchases, Internet browsing, and daydreaming, he can only kill a couple of hours. He could read free online literature—he once stayed late to finish Mary Shelley's Frankenstein in one day—but he's not in the mood.

Ah, an email. The daily corporate announcement sent to everyone in DexiaTel. He scrolls down the message, slowing at one item that begins with those fateful words, "I regret . . .," signalling the cancellation of yet another project. The Telemark Conversion. A simple undertaking to transform data from an older system to a newer one. So simple yet it failed; the older system lives on. Dustin had predicted its doom based simply on the assignation of its prime manager, Chuck Bates. Such accurate prophesying no longer provides much satisfaction though.

On the contrary, to witness project after project turn into miserable failure is painful, especially when he thinks of those unwitting developers who work long hours and weekends to meet impossible, often pointless, deadlines. Deadlines blindly set by scrambling managers trying to impress their superiors or insecure ones reacting to empty escalation threats. At times it seems harder to observe Clay Fortnum's world than to work in it. How things changed when that man became Chief Information Officer.

Clay's first act as CIO was to eliminate the director management level, Dustin's level. The step was hailed at the time for its braveness—even though all the other directors save Dustin had left already—and its organizational efficiency. And so sycophants like Bates and Joyce Morrison and, later on, Joyce Blanton, not to mention Fortnum's architects and the prince of bureaucracy, Jacques Chartrand, suddenly reported directly to the CIO. The poor fools saw it as a promotion, or at the very least, that they were now prodigies. They began to emulate Fortnum's tactics, quoting his utterances without comprehending them, meticulously interpreting every statement—missing obvious contradictions—and then attempting to accommodate them.

Dustin chose not to play that game.

How convenient then for the new CIO when that fateful Melange project came about. Simultaneously, Clay ensured Melange would fail and bring Dustin down. His only error was in assuming Dustin would want to leave.

"Do what's right for you, what's best for you," Fortnum would hint after Melange's end, in an offhand, dispassionate way of poking at Dustin's pride.

Resigning was the dignified thing to do, Dustin knew that, but a certain twitching of Fortnum's mouth betrayed the man's eagerness. So Dustin applied the CIO's advice literally, concluding that leaving was not in his best interest. It was a poor job market for IT people—it still is—so why not continue taking the money? And he still carries hope that one day the department will flourish again. Won't happen with Clay Fortnum in charge, but CIO's, like all executives, are vulnerable. Should that day come, Dustin will be ready.

That day is not today, though. As has become his habit, he leaves early. Just as the nauseating odour of microwave popcorn reaches him, he runs into Rebecca Spencer from Human Resources. An awkward encounter because he knows she knows and she knows he knows she knows all about his situation. His face turns red but she acts as if nothing is unusual and walks past him, leaving Dustin staring out a large window.

The clouds have cleared, the sun is shining through. Several blocks away, beyond the grey and green city park, partially blocked by several low-rise glass office buildings, stands DexiaTel headquarters, where his accomplishments once warranted a window office.

Before Melange.

The blinds are open on the top storey. He can make out little shadowy heads, human movements.

The DexiaTel boardroom occupies the northwest corner of the penthouse at headquarters. Forty-five people can sit wide-elbowed around its magnificent oval oak table in plush brown leather swivel chairs, while another sixty can observe from the more modest cloth-cushioned black chairs that line the walls in an outer horseshoe. A mini art gallery covers the beige walls, an eclectic collection of original paintings and photographs by Canadian artists, all of them abstracts offering occasional amusement but not so engaging as to create a distraction.

Three executives—Charles Wenham, President and Chief Executive Officer; Stu Cairns, Vice President of Operations; and Miranda Fisher, Vice President of Marketing—ponder the conclusions presented by a fourth person, Megan Watson. Megan, Vice President of Complex Solutions at Paleo Transitions, has just given an outline of her company's proposal. She stands at the front, fingers tapping at pursed lips, observing her clients.

Stu appears agitated, his face reddening, highlighting the blondness of his hair. His frown reveals wrinkles in an otherwise youthful face and his bullish body has tensed up. There is much at stake for him, professionally, but Megan senses his motivation is personal too. Unlike Miranda who remains calm, brushing her long auburn hair behind her neck with the back of her hand. Her face, its prettiness marred by a persistent smirk, appears casually indifferent. An incorrect interpretation, Megan knows, and she can see in those dark, penetrating eyes that Miranda is as intensely interested as the other two. Of the three, she will survive whether this fails or succeeds. Not a muscle shifts on Wenham's long poker face as he continues perusing the materials.

"This is drastic," the CEO finally says.

The hesitancy in his voice strikes Megan as affected, as if he needs to show some resistance, to test the others. He ought to test them, because he has the most to lose. Their support is all he has to mitigate his risks.

"We don't want any more fiascos like Melange, do we?" Fisher says.

"Charles, we have no choice," Cairns says. "Firing a few people and performing another reorg won't do the job."

"What do you need from us next?" Wenham says, addressing Megan.

"Aside from one administrative item, nothing. My people are in place and ready to go. From here on, the less you're involved, the better. I recommend we conduct future meetings at the Paleo office."

"Wonderful," Fisher says, "I love that little restaurant you guys have." Then she stands up to close some blinds, blocking the view of the IT building across the way. "But how do you recommend we deal with Fortnum?"

"He's got to go," Cairns says. "The sooner, the better."

"Now hold on, Stu," Wenham says, "we've gone over this and you've made your position clear. His time will come."

"I understand that," Stu says, "but his presence makes it difficult for Jane to execute her plans. She was anxious to hire a counterpart for IT before Fortnum demanded she hire from within DexiaTel, from a list he provided. And the only person within the IT department Jane would consider isn't available. Having seen the list myself, I can't blame her. But without your intervention, Charles, Rebecca says her HR hands are tied and she has to support Clay's wishes on this."

"I'm afraid Jane will have to wait then," Wenham says. "As far as I'm concerned, replacing my CIO too hastily—not to mention forcing him to accept an organizational change against his will—can only cause turmoil, which can only jeopardize our plans. Isn't that right, Megan?"

"Yes, Charles, the turmoil would be disruptive. But jeopardize our plans? I hope I didn't give you that impression. We'd still succeed, it would just take—"

"A little more of Paleo's time and cost?" Stu says, smiling for the first time.

Megan smiles back. "But I do agree with Charles that it's best to hold off on Clay Fortnum for now."

"What if he gets wind of what we're up to in the meantime?" Fisher says, as Cairns nods.

"Please, people, let's not worry about Fortnum," Wenham says, his voice for the first time showing frustration. "I'll deal with him. He won't be a problem."

Megan watches the CEO stare down his two subordinates before they can object further. She's satisfied now. Thrilled even. In her experience, she has never worked with a client whose top three executives, despite these smaller issues, are as involved and focused and in sync as these ones are. It's time to enact a key piece of her plan and Cairns has provided the opening.

"Stu, you mentioned there was someone in IT Jane could work with. Who is that?"

"Dustin Freeman."

"The guy who ran Melange?" Fisher says. "He's still working here?"

"Yes," Cairns says, letting out a forced cough.

"Excuse me," Wenham says. "But are you telling me the leader of that failure is still an employee of DexiaTel?"

"Listen, Charles," Cairns says. "It wasn't Dustin Freeman's fault, not entirely at least, that Melange turned out as it did. But I agree it's not good to have him around. I've told Fortnum for months now, assign him something or get rid of him. He's bound to be a distraction."

"What's holding Clay back?" Megan says.

"I don't know," Stu says, shrugging.

"That Freeman guy was pretty good, no?" Miranda says. "Maybe Clay's got him working on something useful."

"I don't think so," Stu says. "Apparently, Fortnum can't trust Freeman and is unwilling to assign him anything, let alone make him available to Jane. He'll fight to the end to prevent Dustin Freeman gaining any influence in the IT department again."

"Well why wouldn't Freeman just quit?"

Fisher's question hangs awkwardly and even Megan is at a loss to explain this. The Dustin Freeman she used to know would have bolted long ago. Her old friend wasn't the type to hold out for severance, let alone endure not working on anything. It's a troubling notion, possibly an uncertain element in her plan.

"If he won't go on his own, you need to fire him," Megan says. "If there's a way to do it without Fortnum knowing, all the better."

"Why would it matter to you, Megan?" Fisher says.

"If anyone can stumble on to what's going to happen, it's him."

"And how would you know that?" Fisher says, smiling.

"Because he and I once worked together," Megan says," her voice defiant, ready to answer any challenges. Beyond an exchange of glances, none comes.

"I'll get Rebecca Spencer on it," Wenham says.

Paper jam.

Marty Tellerini releases a series of curses under his breath. This would happen just as a meeting is ending with people streaming out. Some slow to greet him but no one lingers to help. Alone again, he opens the uncooperative machine, rips out the spoiled sheet, and slips it into the shredding bin. Back to his desk then to resubmit the file. In a minute, the printer resumes with Marty's hands at the tray ready to snatch the output before anyone can discern its contents.

He needn't worry because everyone seems to have gone for lunch, allowing him to inspect the three concise paragraphs of this fifth draft. Oh, how he wants to say more, much more, pages more in fact. But what would that achieve? He is far too young to be this bitter and it is far too early in his career to burn bridges. Marty signs the bottom, folds it neatly, inserts it into a letter-sized envelope displaying the maroon-and-teal DexiaTel logo. Then he takes a deep breath and marches to his boss's office.

Marty stops to peer through the blinds before knocking, sees Chuck's belly pressing against the desk edge, his left hand blindly fumbling through a bag of Doritos nestled between two piles of documents, his right hand expertly dragging and clicking the mouse. Probably jostling meetings so he can tag along with the IT architects on some offsite vendor seminar, Marty thinks, as he raps on the door and opens it.

"Chuck, can I—?"

"Oh, Marty," Chuck says, sliding his chair back, brushing crumbs from his shirt. "Sorry man, it's not a good time."

"It won't take long."

"I said no. Whatever it is, it'll have to wait a few hours. I'll come by after Clay's meeting. Promise."

Chuck grabs a notebook and brushes past Marty. For some reason, this is not as annoying as it would have been at any other time. Indeed, Marty is actually relieved, as this only strengthens his resolve. Telling Chuck can wait a few hours.

Marty passes by the elevators where he spots Jane Gooden doing up the buttons on her fur coat. He has rarely seen her since Stu Cairns promoted her to Vice President of Business Automation. Her long black hair has been cut, making her stature shorter, but at the same time adding an aura of power to her feistiness.

Jane was one of the first non-IT people Marty met at DexiaTel. Already then she had a chip on her shoulder about the IT department, which strained their relationship at first. Marty's newness to the company, and to the industry for that matter—it was his first job out of college—soon became evident to Jane and she latched on to him after the success of their first project together. From then on, she demanded he be her dedicated IT liaison for all her important projects, and usually got her way. That suited Marty. Jane was the only person from the business capable of making decisions that stuck and succinctly articulating what end-users truly needed. Yet Marty now believes he lost standing with his peers—and particularly with his superiors—in the IT department because of this. Some were envious of his favoured status, and his knack for getting her to agree to his suggestions, while others actually made him feel traitorous. Her recent promotion only promised to isolate him further within his own department.

"Slumming?" Marty says, with a brief chuckle.

"What would you call a half-day meeting with Missy?" she says, with a weary smile. "I'll be glad to get back to my headquarters haven."

"Ouch, Missy—that's rough," says Marty, as the elevator door opens and he follows her in. "What'd she do this time?"

"I've complained about her so often but either your managers are too impotent, too stupid, or too scared of her. Or something else."

"But at your level why would you be dealing with someone like Missy? Can't you delegate?"

"Believe me, I would if I could, but there's a lot of work to do on my side too," Jane says, with a helpless shrug. "A lot of work. But God, how you IT people love your meetings. And why can't a meeting scheduled to end at noon actually end at noon?"

"I know. If we had done more work and had fewer meetings to talk about the work, I'm sure Telemark might have been successful."

"Don't remind me about that one. Between you and me, Marty, my people messed up just as much. If IT cleaned up its act, my problems would be quickly exposed. I'm not ready for that kind of embarrassment yet. Which is why I'll be back and forth a lot, attending these meetings—don't laugh—I mean how could someone as smart as you work for someone like Chuck?"

He stops laughing and shows her the envelope. Just then, the elevator car stops at the fifth floor where three people get on and he deftly slips it behind his back. They keep quiet until they reach the busy concourse where Marty hands it to her.

"Here's how I'm handling it," he says.

She reads the letter, gasps, shakes her head. "You're resigning?"

"You bet. I'm giving that to Chuck later."

"Well, I'm sad to hear it. We'll miss you. I'll miss you but, congratulations. Where are you going? I didn't even know you were looking."

"I wasn't. I'll find something."

"You mean you don't have another job lined up?"

"No, haven't even looked. I know the market's not great, but I'll be okay. Also, this'll send a strong message, don't you think?"

"What message?"

Marty pauses and Jane waits. "I don't know. Someone will—," he says.

She tears up the letter and hands it back to him. "I've a better idea."

0010

Chuck Bates arrives at the eleventh-floor meeting room precisely three minutes before one o'clock and takes his usual seat between the two Joyces, Blanton and Morrison. Morrison is his best friend. Once again she is wearing that frumpy plaid skirt, which makes her square body look even heavier. Blanton, in contrast, is the most attractive woman in the department; she could easily blend in with the women of Sales and Marketing. Her tailored black pantsuit, rather than her normal jeans, indicates she may have a meeting at headquarters. Or maybe she's trying to impress Clay.

On the facing wall hangs a pair of paintings, those nostalgic Toronto winter scenes with the old streetcars. The bobbling heads of Thom, Ron, Carl, Ralph, and a few other IT managers block the wheels and tracks. The architects are present too, all three of them—Ted Scholes, Al Chang, and Fred Holochuk—which is unusual because normally only Fred shows up. Even the tardy and absent-minded Jacques Chartrand from Montreal has already called in, the green light on the black conference device indicating his presence.

Why is everyone so prompt all of a sudden? A nervous tingle creeps through Chuck's belly and he wishes he had brought his Tums. What's next? Will that jerk, Freeman, suddenly show up for one of his dramatic cameos? No, that could never happen now that Clay's banished Dustin to that fifth-floor Siberia. Nothing to fear there, not as long as Fortnum runs the show.

A booming baritone from outside the room announces the imminent arrival of Chuck's boss, Clay Fortnum, DexiaTel's Chief Information Officer.

"Well there's not much we can do if they haven't provided all the information we need, is there? Do they expect us to rely on osmosis?"

The remark draws a few smirks inside the room. Chuck can picture the scene outside, imagine the events leading up to it; relieved to be witness instead of participant. It is also evident Clay intentionally raised his voice for the benefit of those in the room.

Fortnum enters and surveys the filled seats, momentarily distracted by the scribbled notes on the large whiteboard—the same notes have been on the board since before Christmas—but then strolls to the head of the table. The CIO, today in a navy blue suit with pale orange tie, is not a tall man. Joyce Morrison once told Chuck the man's habitual lateness was to ensure he always remains physically above everyone else. Chuck has to admit the ploy works. Whether from reverence or fear, no one makes eye contact with Clay until he takes the empty chair at the head of the table. Several seconds pass during which Fortnum says nothing.

"All right Joyce, let's begin with you," he says, as if unsure of the meeting's purpose.

Joyce Blanton and Joyce Morrison exchange glances across Chuck who shrugs. Joyce Morrison, more senior in age and service, begins.

"My projects are fine, no major issues, all green."

"Good."

"But I do have a situation with Sue Greeley from Network Operations. She keeps pulling one of my best programmers, Dennis, away to answer her questions. They're not simple questions either, but ones that take time to investigate. I'm afraid, if it goes on, it will encroach not only on my projects but on others' too."

Chuck can sympathize. He's worked with Greeley before, has personally suffered from the business manager's manipulations and hasty escalations. But Fortnum only stares at Joyce, his eyes unsympathetic.

"And what does she say to that?"

"She? Who?"

"Sue Greeley," Fortnum says, and flashes an exasperated glance at the architects who grin.

"Well, I haven't—I mean—there's not much point in talking to her. She just doesn't understand how we do things in IT. I wanted to bring it up now, before someone here complains."

"For crying out loud, you're managers. Can't you people control your staff?"

A hush goes over the room. Joyce Morrison is one of Fortnum's pets; it is rare to see her challenged this way.

Chuck, and undoubtedly his peers too, sense that in her misery there may be personal benefit. Chuck shifts his body slightly to put space between them, but then shifts back. He feels for his friend when he catches the desperation in her voice.

"It's not that exactly, it's, well, it's, Dennis does try to resist but Sue's very persuasive. And they go back years, and have developed a strong relationship—don't get me wrong, I think that's a good thing—but it also makes it harder to manage him."

"So what are you going to do about it?" Fortnum says.

The room becomes completely quiet, all eyes on Joyce Morrison. When she fails to answer, Fortnum sighs sharply and makes no effort to hide his frustration.

"I take it you're asking me to intervene and talk to Greeley's superiors?"

Joyce meekly nods.

"All right, I can do that. Anything else?"

Chuck knows she has plenty to bring up, recalling the hour he spent commiserating with her at lunch the day before. Joyce shakes her head. Smart move, Chuck thinks. Her experience with Fortnum is paying off. She knows that next week his mood and responses will probably be different. She leans back, wounded, but not beaten.

Now hostage eyes regard Fortnum with fear and wonder: whom will he target next for execution? Then, as if from some logical instinct, several heads turn to Joyce Blanton. She does not hesitate, her voice confident.

"I've had to put Phase B of Calypso in yellow, and I expect we'll have to red flag it any day now."

Another bout of silence fills the room; declaring a project in trouble so boldly is risky.

"Why?" Fortnum says, calmly.

"The usual, business requirements stability. Almost every day they change their minds on something they were certain about the day before. It's hindering development."

"Ah yes, just what I was talking to Kevin about before the meeting. I apologize if I was a little loud out there."

He pauses. Joyce Blanton, as if done playing her part, sits back and keeps quiet while the CIO leans forward, arms on the table, fists clenched and joined at the knuckles.

"The problem never seems to go away, does it? As I've said before, too often before, do not let your business clients confuse you with their indecisiveness. Or their appeals for urgency. Or their escalation threats. Or any other tactic in their bureaucratic arsenal. Remember, we are the end of the line, the machine end. We have no humans to whom we can shift the blame. A computer is a wonderful thing but it doesn't care a whit about politics. It has no ability to identify or excuse human laziness or incompetence. A computer can't think for them, or for anyone, nor should it, right? You all know the old adage: 'This damn computer, I wish they would sell it; it never does what I want it to, only what I tell it.' For some reason, our business partners have difficulty grasping this."

Clay pauses again, perhaps for a breath, perhaps to ensure no one's attention has drifted from his impromptu speech.

"So from now on, going forward, in all cases, and I mean all cases, we're taking a hard line. Until the business documents the required system changes—explicitly and thoroughly—we cannot, and will not, proceed. That means getting approvals, signoffs from all their key people, whomever they identify at the outset. No exceptions. And make sure you get all the approval names up front. Don't allow a last-second VP or Director So-and-so whack-a-mole to pop up and demand to review and approve it and stall progress. After all, if they can't get formal agreement on their side, how can we be confident about what we build?"

Fortnum exhales dramatically, stands up, removes his jacket, rolls up his sleeves, and walks a circle around the room. Clay is in high form today, Chuck thinks, recalling stories of Al Capone and his baseball bat. The same menace is there, albeit weapon-less. Clay mostly addresses the ceiling and walls as if the room is empty, occasionally clasping the back of Fred Holochuk's chair.

"No wonder they complain about costs when they ask, demand, cajole, or beg us to begin developing before what we are supposed to deliver is known. 'Just go ahead,' they say, 'you know what it is we need.' And then when they inevitably change what they want, midstream, not only do we have to understand what's changed, we have to undo what's done and throw it away. I shudder to think how much this has cost the company over the years."

Fortnum returns to his seat. His face regains pallor as he looks past Chuck and straight at Joyce Blanton. To Chuck's dismay, his pretty colleague is revelling in the exclusive attention.

"Joyce, here's what I want you to do. Arrange a steering committee meeting so I can straighten this out. It has to be within the next two days. Until we have that meeting, you are not to proceed, unless by some miracle the requirements stabilize to your satisfaction. But even if that happens, get my approval first."

She nods, scribbling frantically, but when he stops talking, she looks up as he seems to be searching for words.

"Clay, what about the work that's—?"

"What?"

"Well, in some areas we have—"

"I hope you're not about to tell me you've already begun programming any of this. I don't want to know that."

Her mouth remains open but nothing comes out. Clay stares at her until it closes. She's learning when to keep quiet, Chuck thinks. Everyone knows damn well she's lying and that she's gotten a head start, just as they would have done in her position. Part of him admires and another part resents her blatant ambition, which appears to be effective. Fortnum pulls the telephone closer.

"Jacques?"

The phone emits a guttural sound.

"Yes, Clay, I am here."

"Jacques, update me on the new requirements gathering processes, especially those signoff documents. As you can see, things will only get worse until we formalize our approach on paper. We need this yesterday."

"No problem Clay, we are almost ready. In fact I am in the process of scheduling a meeting with for the end of the week—the end of next week—to review what we have produced."

Chuck and everyone else can sense the gloating in Montreal, just as they know Jacques perceives the envy in Toronto.

"Well, call my admin immediately after this meeting and re-schedule it for first thing tomorrow morning."

Envy turns to relief; gloating to fear.

"But we still need a few days to make some final adjustments."

"C'mon, Jacques, what can you do in a few days that you haven't done in the past six months? I don't care if it's unpolished or needs a bit of proofreading. We'll review what you have. As is. Email all of it—and it had better be substantial—to Trudy, before she leaves today, so she can make copies, all right?"

"Sure, but—"

"What?"

"Yes, today, of course. May I leave the meeting now to attend to that?"

"No. I have to share something with all of you first."

Fortnum leans forward in his chair. Unconsciously Chuck apes his boss's movement, sensing that whatever he is about to hear will resolve his still lingering uneasiness from the beginning of the meeting.

"Folks, I have a couple of announcements. The first is that in a couple of days I will be off to Europe for a technological symposium, followed by a vacation. So I'll be away for several weeks."

"What if issues come up in the meantime that need your approval," Joyce Morrison says.

"I suggest to you," Fortnum says, glaring at her, "that you speak with some of the others here who may have been paying better attention."

He pauses until Joyce nods sheepishly.

"Now then, there's another matter. As you've all probably heard, Stu Cairns recently created, under Jane Gooden, a new position—a director level position no less—specifically to address what they see as a deteriorating IT / Business partnership. I personally don't see any benefit to this but I'm a team player and so I've agreed to establish a corresponding position within my department."

A murmur runs through the room; this is the first inkling of advancement since the merger.

"I've provided Ms. Gooden with a list," Clay continues, "with the names of everyone at this meeting and, in the spirit of good relations, agreed to allow Jane to select who that person will be. Now, I must admit, she wasn't fully receptive to the list at first, thought it should have contained some more names, including the name of one individual we need not mention here."

Then he pauses to glance at Chuck and smiles.

"She also suggested I include Marty Tellerini."

"Oh?" Chuck says, his voice dry.

"Should I include him? She made a decent argument."

"Ah, no," Chuck says, but then gains his composure. "Of course not. He's not experienced enough."

"Right," Clay says, and then looks away, signalling the end of the meeting.

0011

The next morning when Marty visits Chuck there is no mention of his manager's promise to see him after Clay's meeting, let alone an apology. After lukewarm pleasantries, Marty hands his boss a piece of paper and sits down, his clammy hands clasping and unclasping on his lap belying the calm confidence he feels inside. Chuck reads the letter and his eyes alternately widen in surprise then squint as if reading hieroglyphics. Marty is not sure whether this reaction is genuine or a delay tactic. It comes as a liberating relief to realize how little that matters.

"Is this what I think it is?" Chuck says, finally.

"At the moment, I'm not really happy about things."

"Oh?" Chuck says, rising slightly. "Not happy? Not happy about what?"

"For one thing, I put in a lot of effort on the Telemark Conversion and I guess the cancellation's gotten me down. I mean, it was a pretty straightforward project."

"You're too sensitive, Marty. It was just a project and some projects tend to fail."

"It seems a lot of projects tend to fail around here."

"Now listen—"

"No, Chuck, I didn't come here to get into an argument. Maybe I just need a break. A little time to think about it all."

Chuck's lips twitch briefly before his expression resumes its original impassiveness. He picks up the piece of paper again and looks at it as if there is more to it. Now he turns to his computer where he performs a couple of mouse clicks, perhaps consulting an electronic oracle. Chuck has evolved his stalling techniques well and it frustrates Marty to endure them.

"The form's all filled out, is there something else you need?" Marty says.

"I'm not sure. This is the first leave of absence request I've ever received." Then Chuck frowns. "What about your projects?"

"Cancelled, remember? And Telemark's not likely to resurface again, according to Jane's announcement."

"Jane Gooden, ah yes," Chuck says, his voice carrying an odd inflection. "She's getting pretty comfy in her new role, isn't she? I wonder what she's—hey, you're pretty good friends with her, aren't you?"

"Why?" Marty says.

"Never mind. Okay, who's going to be your backup when you're gone?"

"Backup? Isn't it your job to assign a backup? Besides, I'm an analyst. I don't support anything operational."

"Everyone's got to have a backup arranged if they leave, no matter how short or how long. Those are Clay's rules, not mine."

"But what would they back up? I have no projects."

Marty sighs as a superior smile crosses Chuck's face; the only way forward for him is to play this game.

"You still need to put a name down."

"Maybe you could help me out with that," Marty says.

"I can't promise anything but I'll see what I can do," Chuck says.

Marty nods and then leaves, still confident he's made the right decision, but also frustrated by Chuck's inability or unwillingness to deal with it immediately.

Chuck saunters into Joyce Morrison's office, closes the door behind him.

"Lunch is on me today," he says, gleefully. "I got Tellerini out of the way."

Usually pleased to see him, Joyce now pays him little attention, perhaps still sore about the last meeting with Clay. Chuck plops down in the chair across from her. Joyce's desk is tidy, with only her computer, an opened binder, and a pencil caddy. That's always bothered him. But he's too pleased with his good fortune to let her desk or her mood put him off. Chuck sits silently until she pushes in her keyboard and gives him her attention.

"Did you hear what I said?" he says.

"I've got ears." Chuck smiles and keeps silent, knowing she's taunting him with her indifference. "Okay, I'll bite," she says. "How'd you manage it?"

"Actually, I didn't have to do anything. He requested a leave of absence."

"Really? For how long?"

"Only six weeks."

"I'm impressed. That's perfect. Long enough for him to find a job somewhere else."

"You think that's what he's going to do?"

"I know Chuck, it's hard to believe someone would want to leave Your Majesty's kingdom for another, but you'll be better off without his kind."

"What do you mean?"

"Nothing, forget it. Did you get Fortnum's approval? If not, you'd better do so before he's gone."

Chuck shifts irritably in his seat and sniffs; he never likes reminders of the limits of his authority. Not having dealt with this situation before, he'd forgotten such a move needs the CIO to sign off.

"He'll okay it, won't he?"

"Beats me, Chuck. But what about Blanton? She's about to kick-off Phase B of her Calypso project. Weren't you going to assign Marty to replace Phil for that?"

"Damn it, I forgot Phil left."

"Relax, you can always get a contractor."

"Too expensive and it's too big a learning curve for such a complex project."

A quiet minute passes until Joyce's lips and eyebrows rise simultaneously to form a crude smile.

"I've got your answer for you. And I'm surprised you didn't think of it."

"Think of what?"

"Why, Missy, of course."

"Missy?"

"Sure, throw her on the project. It got that other one killed, didn't it?"

"But she's a technical analyst, not a business analyst."

"Oh, come on, she's neither a technical analyst nor a business analyst. Of course, according to her she's both and everything else in between, at least until she gets in over her head. Then she just nags and annoys the real developers and tasks them into doing the things she should, but can't. Really, I adore her, she's as useful as poison. Let her do her thing and soon enough everything will be so confused no one will have time to even remember her role."

"That's good, that's very good. I like it. But, won't it harm our friend, the lovely Ms. Blanton?"

"Are you kidding? First of all, Joyce Blanton is not as lovely as all you boys think. Stop blushing. And talk about being in way over her head. But at least she knows it and I'll give her credit for that. With Missy around and drawing all the attention, our friend Ms. Blanton can appear in control and still stay out of the way. She'll be forever grateful."

Slowly Chuck's smile matches hers. "How grateful?"

"Oh, get your mind out of the gutter. Believe me, not that grateful. All kidding aside, Chuck, move fast. Do it today. Skip lunch, if you can. And then, if it works out, don't announce anything until after Marty's gone."

Despite his hunger, Chuck follows Joyce's advice, glad to save a few bucks on treating his friend. His run of good luck continues when Fortnum instantly approves the leave of absence request. Then Missy eagerly accepts the new assignment when Thom Sturm readily agrees to reduce her role on his project. At the end of the day, Chuck silently pronounces Joyce Morrison a genius, when Joyce Blanton's reaction is as exactly as his best friend predicted.

Late in the afternoon, his hunger becomes overbearing, made worse by the smell of microwave popcorn permeating the floor. But he needs something more solid than popcorn. He is thinking about what he can get at the concourse eatery when his office door opens abruptly, banging the wall. He looks up and feels a lump in his throat as his voice cracks.

"Jane, to what do I owe this honour? Are you here to discuss with me this new role that's been created? Clay told us about your plans to—"

"Cut the crap, Chuck. Do not put that woman on Calypso."

"What are you talking—?"

"You know damn well what this is about: Missy Patenkoffel."

"But how did you find out?"

"Who cares? Just remove her from the project."

"Listen, Jane, who are you to tell me—never mind, you should take this up with Joyce Blanton, not me, she's your IT contact for the project."

"I have and she sent me to you."

"That's because she's happy to have Missy. Marty's no longer available, which I'm sure you already know too.

Therefore, I'm afraid I have no one else, not that I'd reassign it anyway. You're going to have to work with Missy."

"I've seen what she does to projects and I'd rather have no one."

"That's a bit harsh, don't you think? I don't see why you'd have a problem with her. She's one of our most versatile analysts, just the type of person this project needs."

"Yeah, right," Jane says, and departs.

Alone again, Chuck sits back, a nervous yet exhilarating feeling running through him from his first successful confrontation with this woman. He then indulges in the darkly wonderful realization that Missy will drive Jane Gooden nuts.

This satisfaction lasts only until he goes to the snack machines and returns with a Pepsi and a bag of Doritos. He's halfway through the bag when he realizes how he and Joyce Morrison never chatted about the new position Clay had announced. Had Joyce avoided the subject on purpose? Did she suggest he assign Missy to get Jane pissed off at him, to get him out of the way? Would his friend do such a thing? He takes a long sip of the Pepsi but then his stomach rumbles so much he has to reach for the Tums.

From the back of the room, Jane struggles to follow the buzzwords coming out of the mouth of Chuck's versatile analyst as Missy, with her curly red hair and perky freckles on her chubby face, rambles through the issues. Before Missy's arrival a week before, there were barely four pages of outstanding issues. Now there are eight and next week there likely will be sixteen.

Part of Jane's new role—the time-consuming dreary part—involves observing what's going on, but doing so by taking a longer view. Meaning she has to restrain her anger and not turn pit bull on every matter. Meaning she'll have to forfeit some battles, perhaps plenty of battles, before she can even hope to win the war. This Calypso project—Phase B—is a challenging one, primarily because in Phase A they deferred all the difficult stuff. She foresees a Phase C and possibly a D as well.

Joyce Blanton, supposedly the one in charge of Calypso, is conspicuously absent. However, there's Chuck, looking bored, occasionally glancing up from his BlackBerry to observe Jane. Lately, he's made a point of showing up at all meetings she attends. Clay's other managers do it too, but not as overtly as Bates. No matter how spur of the moment her decision to attend a meeting is, he somehow gets wind of it. It's a tiny consolation to Jane that, while with her, he is unable to inflict his incompetence on another project.

"On issue thirty-three, we're still waiting for the business to clarify requirements," Missy says.

Issue thirty-three. Jane's personally familiar with that one, a spill over from Phase A. That may be why her people are so reticent; they're afraid to say something wrong in front of her. How disappointing. She needs stronger, less fearful people working for her. Until that happens, she'll continuously have to attack Clay's people, to deflect the weaknesses within her own team.

Sometimes she feels sorry for the IT folks, many of whom are capable and cooperative and innocent victims of her wrath. It must be hard to work with the outcasts from the various business departments that treat their computer systems as a necessary nuisance. Jane intends to revolutionize that situation but she needs Stu's help.

It's becoming tougher to remain patient with her Vice President. He keeps promising he'll convince the other executives to give her power. What's so hard? Why can't she just get Dustin on board? Or hire someone outside DexiaTel? But no, Stu's asked her to avoid the one IT manager worth keeping. She still feels that way about Dustin, despite the mess he allowed Melange to become.

"Now for issue thirty-four, I need—"

"Hold on, hold on," Jane says, her voice jarring Chuck's attention away from his BlackBerry. "Back to thirty-three. I personally know we closed this in the first phase. Why are you bringing it up now?"

Missy, not intimidated, seems to have expected this reaction.

"Yes, Jane, you're right. And closing it was the right decision at that time. However, since then, we've discovered that that fix may not be the best solution for all aspects of that function and that there may be other options. So, really, we're back at square one with this item."

Jane's irritated less by Missy's explanations than the cheerfully condescending manner in which she offers them, as if implying this discovery is good news.

"As far as I'm concerned," Jane says, "the issue is closed. End of story. You, me, all of us will work with the solution agreed to back then and move on." Missy shrugs helplessly, as if to say no one can control the impossible. Chuck remains mute but attentive. Jane struggles to maintain calmness in her voice. "We've developed our business processes and our training based on that decision. There's no time to change it, let alone coordinate the resources again."

"But I'm afraid we can't do it your way," Missy says.

"Why the hell not?"

"Well, for one thing, we're limited by how the current system works," Missy says.

Jane's tempted to point out the limits seem to have more to do with the people working on the project, and not the system itself, but it would be futile and undignified, considering her position.

"How?" Jane says.

"How, what do you mean, how?" Missy says.

"How is it that we are limited by the system?" Jane says.

Missy hesitates, looks at Chuck. He puts down his BlackBerry. "It's complicated," he says.

Jane perks up like a fisherman feeling a tug on the line.

"In what way?"

"It's technical. The explanation would be much too involved to get into at this type of meeting."

"Give me an abridged version. Dumb it down."

"All right, if you insist. It has to do with how our systems were originally developed and how they've evolved over the years. So even small fixes like this can prove significant upon further investigation."

"So because of your short cuts, I have to suffer now."

"That's an unfair and simplistic characterization."

Before she can respond, Chuck undertakes the type of long-winded explanation she has heard too often from technical people who should be working at their desks rather than attending meetings, a verbal cocktail of obscure terms, acronyms, clichés, euphemisms, given in a clinical yet condescending tone intended to both mollify and confuse the listener, but mostly to deter further queries.

"You'll have to trust us on this," he concludes. Then, as if taking Jane's silence as surrender, his voice becomes conciliatory. "But Missy, we need to treat Jane's concerns seriously and ensure we apply due diligence on this issue such that her team can work with the altered solution. Perhaps you can arrange a separate meeting for this?"

"Sure thing," Missy says.

Jane feels helpless. Sure, she can try to continue the fight. With only a scrap of her intelligence, and a great deal of energy and patience, she would win this particular point. While it may give her satisfaction, behind this issue a dozen more like it await. So she says nothing and sits back.

The meeting resumes and once attention turns away from her, Jane quietly exits. In the hallway, she senses Chuck coming up behind her. She quickens her pace but he is persistent and in a few seconds overtakes her, trying not to huff as he catches his breath. He gives her a boyish smile.

"Jane, I feel bad about that issue but situations like that are inevitable. We are trying our best to meet your requirements, but we have our constraints."

"Chuck, I don't believe a single word you say and if, for once, you were honest with yourself, you'd understand why."

Chuck's face is blank, stunned, but he does not appear offended. In fact, Jane cannot ever recall Chuck showing offence. He's like a robot programmed to process criticism through some delusional logic engine, an engine that rationalizes and reverses negativity into self-congratulation, discarding the remainder.

"You know that we're only trying to fulfill your wishes."

"You know what I wish for, Chuck? I wish for people who can work with us on a solution, instead of spending their time coming up with ways to tell us what they can't do. People with the passion to get things done."

"We have passion," Chuck says.

"Passion? Really? Okay, maybe so. But it's a passion without imagination. It's easy to argue passionately for taking the safest course of action, to cry out the need for risk assessments for the smallest decisions."

"You're right," he says, and now she stops and turns around. "You're right. We need to improve things. That's why I think Stu chose you for that role. I want to help."

"You want a promotion, Chuck, that's all."

"Sure I do. But I think I've earned it. Speaking of which, are you close to making a decision?"

His pleading voice is so pathetic. At times like this she regrets making the announcement. Jane wants to put him out of his misery and tell him that she'll never consider him, or any of the others on Clay's list. If it comes to the point when she's forced to choose, Jane's not sure what she'll do. Until then, she'll put it off, weaving other options in her mind.

"No, Chuck, I haven't made a decision yet."

"Okay," he says, and then his broad face widens in a smile as he toddles off.

0100

This has to be the feeblest career fair I've ever attended, Marty thinks, as he strolls along the thick, colourful carpet of the three-star hotel, indifferently passing small, hastily assembled kiosks and flea market style tables. So unlike the years leading up to Y2K when these events took place in grand halls of fancy hotels and lasted three days, not one. One could visit dozens of elegant booths hosted by smiling, attractive representatives, proudly bearing logos of stable, independent companies on badges, golf shirts, crests and business cards. The competition between companies for talent was fierce then, positions offered on the spot, along with signing bonuses, guaranteed annual performance payouts, moving expenses, and other meaningful incentives. Now, with all the Y2K refugees around, it's become a buyer's market. Salaries have decreased and Marty will be lucky if he finds a job paying eighty percent of what he makes at DexiaTel. Nonetheless, he leaves a few resumes with the pathetic optimism of a novel writer sending a query to a publisher.

Of course, many organizations avoid job fairs now and rely on the Internet, either using public job search sites or developing internal HR applications. Marty has tried them but with little success. Oh, he's received many responses but few match the criteria he provides. A big problem with internal sites is that they filter out candidates before a human being has a chance to see them. His lack of a university degree, for instance, now more and more a stated essential requirement, makes Marty a victim of these filters. He shudders to think how many good people are passed over. Maybe citing DexiaTel as his current employer is a filter.

While waiting at the coat check, Marty concedes it's time to try Sam Kraaling. Up till now he's put off calling the headhunter who negotiated his current job. That's because so many organizations recruiting internally to save costs, any association with Sam might get in the way of opportunities rather than find them. Not only that, to Marty, using the same agent to arrive and leave seems unethical; Sam might even have a policy about such situations. But that would be Sam's problem and, with time running out on his leave of absence, what does he have to lose?

The small recruiting firm operates out of a rundown building just outside downtown. Marty enters into the tiny reception area but finds the desk unoccupied. He pokes his head into the narrow hallway behind it and then walks along the creaky floor, passing several noisy and disorganized rooms. In each, people type busily at workstations, side by side, an IT version of a sweatshop. Finally, he reaches Sam's office where the headhunter welcomes Marty with a strong, hearty handshake, invites him in and then closes the door. Everything becomes quiet again.

"Sit down, sit down," Sam says. "What brings you by?"

Marty tells him about his leave of absence and attempts to find work. At the mention of his career fair and Internet forays, Sam winces.

"Don't waste your time with lotteries, son. You should have called me earlier."

"So you have something?"

"Actually, not really, not now. The market's not good and it's hitting me hard. Those people in the other room. They're unemployed programmers. I'm taking on outsourcing work just to get revenue."

"I see," Marty says, unsure if Sam's going to offer him to do the same thing. He doesn't.

"But listen Marty, you never know when something'll come up. This afternoon I'm meeting a potential client for a drink. I'll keep you in mind and let you know."

Well, better than nothing, Marty thinks, as he takes the subway home from Sam's office. Yet not enough to prevent an intense feeling of dread. It seems inevitable he will have to return to DexiaTel, and to Chuck.

But maybe it won't be so bad. When Jane talked him out of quitting, she hinted that there could be something for him in her department. How unusual it would be for someone from IT to transfer to the business, rather than the other way around. The irony appeals to Marty, as does imagining the look on Chuck's face. But whether he ends up with Jane, or has to go back to Chuck, he is glad she intervened when she did. Resigning would have been disastrous.

The phone is ringing when he enters his apartment. Someone from a company called Paleo Transitions. They want to talk with him, want him to come to their offices. He cannot remember the name from the career fair or from his online searches, or from anywhere else. It certainly couldn't involve Sam, because a headhunter would never allow a potential employer to call a recruit directly. Curiosity, more than hope, makes him agree to see them right away.

Paleo Transitions's seven-story office building is located a subway ride, two bus connections, and a ten-minute walk away, in an industrial area close to a highway exit. The modern structure blends in with several others like it, grey steel and tinted glass, at once warm, sleek, and foreboding. Aside from a nondescript restaurant on the main floor, its only tenant appears to be Paleo Transitions. There is no directory. A security guard greets Marty, signs him in, and escorts him to the elevator. An attractive woman, about ten years older than Marty, is waiting for him when the elevator doors open on the seventh floor.

"Marty Tellerini, I'm Megan Watson," she says, in an elegant combination of casualness and professionalism.

Her office is modest compared to those of the DexiaTel vice presidents, although the desk, sofa, table and four chairs look expensive. Their thin chrome supports appear fragile but do not give when he sits down. A large window overlooks the highway along which the little cars and trucks appear to slide, eastbound, westbound, in mesmerizing patterns. Nothing in the room seems ostentatious yet it has an aura of wealth and success.

"Marty, tell me why you want to leave DexiaTel?"

The abruptness of the question startles him. He intended to demand how she got his name but that doesn't seem relevant or appropriate now. He thinks back to the words on the early, longer drafts of his resignation letter, but they now sound petty to him.

"I just do," he says.

"You don't like the work?" Megan says.

"No, that's not quite it. The work is fine for the most part. I mean, there's a lot of skunk work but there's interesting and challenging stuff too. A few of the people are capable and pleasant to work with. The thing is everything we do fails and no one seems to care. In fact, in some cases, I suspect failure is the goal. It's not exactly what I'd expected, coming out of school."

"And what did you expect? What drew you into IT in the first place? Specifically, what made you become a business analyst?"

"I know systems well. I'm good with people. The relationship—"

The phone behind Megan rings. She puts up a finger for Marty to hold that thought, presses a button on the phone, and then bids him to continue. The indication he is more important than all her phone calls impresses him, activating a likewise desire to impress her.

"You were saying," she says.

"Yes, well, the relationship between the IT department and the business is terrible but I still believe it can be fixed. I guess, in the end, I just want to develop systems and improve the company, and work with people. You know, just do my job, and get paid reasonably well. At DexiaTel, the IT department's narrow-minded bureaucracy gets in the way."

"So it's all IT's fault?"

"Yes, I mean, no. To be honest, much of what people in IT complain about our clients is valid. Many business people I work with take advantage of our faults, exploit them as an easy outlet to cover up their own inadequacies. Don't get me wrong. I don't think they set out to antagonize us, at least not initially. Truth is, they are horribly understaffed, spread too thin, while in IT we seem to have an abundance of people. You should see some of the meetings. There's like four IT people for every business representative. And my peers and I have to share those representatives among various projects and they become overloaded. When that happens, they panic and escalate to deflect attention away. It's rather childish."

Megan nods, but seems ready to let Marty continue. His need to unload overcomes his self-consciousness.

"But I can only control my area and do my best. Sure, their requirements—I hate that word—requirements. It sounds as if we're fulfilling an order rather than collaborating to develop a system, an asset. It may sound pointless to make an issue out of a label, a word, but I don't think so."

"Oh really?"

"Here's the thing. It's as if the label—requirement—drives how we run our respective departments. That we've become fixated on the term and adapted everything else to that term instead of the other way around."

"How's that?"

"Now our IT department is no longer in the business of developing and maintaining systems. It's in the business of satisfying requirements, or looking like we do."

"Doesn't that amount to the same thing?"

"It could, I suppose. But sadly, the requirements, or the interpretations of those requirements, are usually a mess. Either they're poorly considered, recorded, and rushed, or so excessive that they are useless to even consider, let alone develop. It wouldn't be so bad if we helped them. And I try to, even though I get my wrists slapped by my peers and my superiors, and sometimes even by the client I'm working with."

"You've put quite some thought into this, Marty. But in a nutshell . . ."

"Well, to me, IT, as well as certain business people, seems to have forgotten they exist to support the business, and instead act like it's the other way around."

"You mean that without IT there would still be a business?"

"Exactly. And without a business, there would be no IT."

They exchange smiles. Marty imagines this is how two academics must feel when at last reaching consensus. He's enjoying this. Yet it's still just talk and now he gets the sense this meeting, just like all his efforts, will lead to nothing.

Suddenly Megan's face turns serious.

"Your company is an extreme. There are better places, Marty. And much worse too."

"Worse than DexiaTel? I mean, what kind of place would have a guy like Dustin Freeman, whom I've heard good things about, and who many of my peers liked working with, just sitting around doing nothing."

"You don't know him yourself?"

"All I know is there was some kind of controversy about him just after I joined."

"Controversy?"

"Some massive project no one likes to talk about. It happened before I joined so I'm afraid I don't know the details. But wait, you know him?"

28

"As a matter of fact, Dustin's an old friend of mine, someone I worked with years ago, at another company. It surprises me that you two have worked in the same place and never met. You remind me of him in a number of ways and I'm sure you two would work well together."

"Well, if that's true, then I'm not surprised. I know my manager, as well as his peers, and they make an effort to keep like minds apart."

"They would do that?"

"Perhaps I'm giving them too much credit. Instinctively, maybe."

Megan seems amused by this. "Tell me Marty, if DexiaTel operated along the ideal lines you and I have just talked about, would you leave?"

"Wait a minute. Did you want to talk to me because of my resume or because I work at DexiaTel?" Megan says nothing, her expression blank. "And you haven't yet told me what Paleo Transitions does."

"I haven't? Well, essentially, we fix IT departments."

"You fix? Hold on, is DexiaTel your client?" Again, she remains quiet, watching him, like a teacher waiting for her pet student to work out a difficult problem. "That would explain why Chuck and his gang are acting so strangely."

"Strangely?" she says, for the first time appearing startled. "In what way?"

"Aha, so something is going on?" Marty says. "What is it? Is Fortnum going?"

"Marty, as a fellow professional, can I ask that you keep our discussion to yourself?"

He pauses. Maybe that's what she meant by calling him a professional, one with the sense of knowing this is a time to keep quiet, to trust.

"Who would I tell?" he says, shrugging.

"I'm glad we had this talk, Marty."

"Me too. But let me be clear. If there's something happening, and if you can swing it, I want to be involved. I want to help."

Hours later, he realizes he never discovered how she found him. Of course, if DexiaTel were a Paleo Transitions client, there would be numerous ways for her to find him, an idea chilling and exciting at the same time. Maybe she was only mining for information about his company. Otherwise, why would someone so busy have spent so much time talking about the other stuff, gaining his respect and confidence?

Spirit lifting as the experience was, though, it still led to nothing. The next day, reluctantly, Marty makes the call he hoped he wouldn't have to make, but in a sense always knew he would.

Chuck hangs up the phone and, beneath a dramatic sigh, swears, just as Joyce Morrison enters his office.

"That's the last thing I need right now," he says, as she sits down.

"What is it now, Chuck?"

"Marty. He wants to come back two weeks early from his sabbatical. Personnel tells me I have to let him."

"That's a shame. And just after Calypso got cancelled."

"Don't remind me. The timing couldn't be worse for my credibility. Not only that, Clay'll be back any day now. With my luck, Jane will hear about this and let me have it soon."

"Speaking of Jane, do you think she's come to a decision yet?"

"You'd know before I would, Joyce," Chuck says, his voice petty.

"Oh, not that Missy thing again. You really believe I'd sabotage your chances for promotion like that—no, no, don't you dare look at me that way. That project was going to fail with or without Missy. And Joyce Blanton's the one who'll take the hit. You're fine."

"I think both of us have taken the hit. Well done."

Joyce shakes her head.

"Don't sulk, Chuck. What option did you have? Would you have offered Marty a raise to make him stay? And then fight with Clay to honour it?"

"No."

"Okay then, let's forget about Jane for a moment. What are you going to do with him? Do you have work for him?"

Joyce takes out her nail file and begins attacking her fingers. They remain silent for several minutes.

"Hey," Chuck says, "maybe I can get him fired—I mean packaged out of here."

Joyce raises her eyebrows, sniggers softly, and then puts her nail file away. "Well, knowing Clay as I do," she says, "I wouldn't dare take a request like that to him. The way he's watching our finances, a severance expense would make him flip. And Marty's still headcount. Clay doesn't want his department to shrink."

"Yeah, you're right. I'll have to take him back, I guess."

"But don't forget who controls his assignments. If you do it right he may want to leave, on his own. I'm sure there must be some process documentation, some committee to head, or some other busywork that you can throw at him. Jacques could dig up something."

"Hey, that's a great idea."

"Of course it is. It's your only option. Maybe his timing isn't so bad after all. Since we have so few projects, it'll also be easier to keep him from Jane and her gang. Once you bury him in Jacques's world no one will find him."

"What if someone demands he replace someone on one of the current projects? I hear Marketing's got a slew of new ones coming up."

"Chuck, really, I'm surprised at you. This is kid's stuff, especially for a manager of your experience and stature."

Chuck nods, but inside his stomach churns, unsure he is up to Joyce's estimation. Yet she is right in that her suggestion is the only option he has. Unless she's playing him again.

0101

The three DexiaTel executives nod enthusiastically during Megan's status report, which shows how their future IT department will blend with the rest of the company organizationally, operationally, geographically. Many of the details the ostrich-like executives seem a bit too happy to leave in Paleo's hands. This lack of inquisitiveness troubles Megan.

"Jane Gooden is ready anytime," Stu says. "In fact, she's rather anxious, so your people will find her accommodating."

"But she's not aware of the overall objective yet, is she?" Megan says, not hiding her concern.

"No, but I keep promising her change. If I don't show something soon, I'm afraid she might resign."

"Soon enough she'll be let in on it, but not yet," Megan says.

"Don't worry," Miranda says, with a grin. "My people will keep her and everyone distracted. I've got plenty of new products lined up, all requiring system changes."

Always a wild card in any telecommunications organization, Megan never expected DexiaTel's Marketing VP to be as supportive in this effort as she has been. Of course, it's easy for Miranda now because she will not experience the pain until later on, when stronger procedures will curtail her ambitious plans. By then it will be too late to retreat. Megan wonders if Miranda realizes that.

"Now Charles, we are behind on one important item," Megan says.

"You mean Freeman, don't you?" Cairns says, before Wenham can respond. "Again, my concern is Jane. You see, she and Freeman are, or at least were, good friends. I'm not sure how she'll respond to his dismissal."

This comes as news to Megan and she mentally notes to check later whether it will make a difference to her plan. Megan asks, "Does Jane even have to know?"

"It would be hard to keep something like that from spreading."

"Megan," Miranda says, "I thought at first you only wanted him out of the way because he could disrupt our plans, but now I sense he'll be involved in this, somehow."

Megan smiles, but says nothing and waits for the question.

"So why make DexiaTel pay for a severance package, which to me seems a pointless expense? Why not hire him yourself?"

"Does it really matter how it's done?" Wenham says.

"Actually Charles, it does matter," Megan says. "Imagine Fortnum's reaction, or Jane Gooden's, for that matter, if it came out that Dustin left to work for my company?"

"Precisely," Wenham says. "Let me assure you the matter's being taken care of as we speak."

Dustin exits DexiaTel for the last time, carrying only a manila envelope. He has no personal effects, having long ago prepared for Rebecca Spencer's late morning visit. At least DexiaTel offered a decent severance payout. He could have bargained for more, even though he'd have accepted less.

The amount isn't important, though. Winning the corporate game of chicken over Fortnum, on the other hand, is a satisfying victory, albeit a vain one. Especially as the CIO couldn't do it himself but had to hide behind HR. The meeting with Rebecca—who appeared rather sad and frazzled—was surprisingly bland. After months of rehearsing opinions and recommendations for improvement, all for the possibility someone might one day ask, no one did. There was no formal exit interview, no grilling about what led to this, no attempt to understand his perspective, no reproach. He would be gone and forgotten soon enough. Unfortunately, it might take longer the other way around. Freed from this misery, and slightly wealthier, Dustin finds himself still bloated with acrimony but no opportunity to vent, let alone any hope of ever implementing his long-simmering changes.

At home, Dustin turns his attention to the future. He digs up his address book and begins to make calls. It's been some time since he's spoken with many of these people and the reactions, even from the headhunters, range from lukewarm to cold. Has Fortnum blacklisted him? The thought makes him stop.

Two blocks from his home is Reggie's, the pub he used to frequent before he took the job at Celsus, in the good days before the merger. Nostalgia seems an unlikely antidote for his gloom but what the hell.

The dark décor has not changed from the days he joined Megan Watson and others there after work. The pool tables and dartboards are in the same place and, like him, a little worse for years of wear. The bartender is new, as are the waitresses. In another era, his beer would be in front of him at his regular table before his coat was off. That table is occupied today, so Dustin takes a stool at the bar, orders a Guinness, which he sips slowly.

What next?

He'll have to polish up his resume. His qualifications will shine but how will he account for these unproductive past months. In a face-to-face interview, will the accumulated bitterness seep out and put off prospective employers? Dustin might come off no better than those prima donnas who've always annoyed him. His attempts to explain may be interpreted as self-pitying, subversive, insubordinate, and petty. All those idle months, lamenting over his past, letting resentment fester instead of planning his future, a psychological stain on an otherwise impressive career.

Dustin observes the two well-dressed men occupying his old table. Between burger bites and soda sips they each leaf through a thick binder. One of the men closes his and Dustin recognizes the DexiaTel logo on the cover. But they are not employees. Vendors probably, a sales guy and his most eloquent technical support guy. The one leafing through the pages appears agitated.

"Check out this piece of crap," he says. "Two thousand pages on the data interface. It's like reading Joyce."

"Who?"

"James Joyce. Stream of conscious—never mind."

"Is it really that bad?"

"I think this is an internal document, which they just passed on, as is. Seriously, I don't think we have the time to go through it."

"Well, someone will have to because we can't lose this account. It's a cash cow."

"When's our bid due?"

"Two weeks."

"I don't see how—"

"Listen, can't you just work with whoever wrote it?"

"Al Chang? That guy's the biggest problem. Him and his Siamese twin, Holochuk. You met them, the architects who divine the future but can never give a direct answer. Just a half hour of words and slides of convoluted designs that confuse you more."

"Yeah, but their confusion's good business for us," says the second man, and his laugh causes Dustin to smile too.

"You don't care if we help them out or not, do you?"

"Sure I do, sure I do."

"And what's worse is how defensive they get about this document. It's an unreadable mess but they think it's as clear as a children's story."

"All right, I'll talk to the guy in charge. What was his name again? Battis?"

"Bates, and good luck. Even more useless than the guy who wrote this."

An impulse tempts Dustin to offer his services as a consultant to these guys, a former insider who knows all the ins and outs of DexiaTel. But some force keeps him from walking over there, some instinct he cannot question, only follow. The urge diminishes then vanishes with another beer, and another . . .

The one-drink-before-the-train-home crowd has left and it's dark outside now. His old table is empty again, but only for a moment, as a striking, confident woman takes it, bringing along her beer glass. This could be a good omen, Dustin thinks, this may turn out to be an interesting evening.

He continues to watch her out of the corner of his eye. She drinks her beer slowly, both palms around her mug in a way that strikes him as familiar. When the woman catches his gaze, she smiles, and the face turns into Megan Watson's, an older, more serious looking Megan.

0110

Now that he's seen her, Megan stands up. They hug warmly for several seconds before taking seats across from each other. For such old friends, the reunion is unusually awkward, similar to that evening, years ago, when they almost took their friendship too far. They got past that then, somehow, Megan recalls, and will do so this time too. A waitress comes by and Megan orders a pitcher. Dustin nods toward the entrance.

"Should we order several?" he says. "In case Val and Gil walk in."

"Have you even been in touch with the old gang lately?"

Dustin's frown reveals the despair in his face; things have gone badly for him. Unlike Marty Tellerini, who is younger and more resilient, the situation at DexiaTel may have permanently scarred Dustin. And, knowing him as she does, combined with what she's heard from Marty and Stu, a certain amount of self-destruction is involved too. Including him in her plans could be a bigger risk than she originally thought.

"You'll be happy to hear I'm no longer at Celsus, I mean, DexiaTel," he says.

"Oh? Why should that make me happy?"

"I haven't forgotten what you said back then."

"I don't even remember what I said," Megan says. A lie; she can recall word for word her warnings.

"You said, 'Don't let the large salary, bonuses, parties, conventions, and other perks of the Telecom world distract you from the reality. You're jumping into a mix of poorly designed systems built with immature methodologies and managed by prematurely promoted managers.' Or something like that."

"Was I right?"

"More than you know. How ironic that the most technically leading-edge companies are often the most archaic internally. It took me a while to realize that I had transported back in time, that their methodologies were a generation behind."

"And now."

"And now, the gap is even greater. They're regressing. But to me what's worse is the complete indifference to the actual people who use the systems. I remember so clearly my first week when I asked several people in IT about visiting our clients, seeing our systems in action and meeting the people who used them. Each one looked at me as if I was insane. I laughed it off at the time but I should have treated it as a clear sign of what was to come. More likely, I deluded myself to think I could make a difference."

"You're being too hard on yourself."

"No, I don't think so," he says, then pauses to order another pitcher. "It's wonderful to see you again, Megan."

He's halfway loaded, she realizes. Might be good to let him release his pent-up frustration, get it out of his system. He probably hasn't had anyone to talk to in a long time.

"The funny thing, Megan, is that for a few years there, it wasn't all bad. There were others in the department, and the company, with views similar to mine. Like me, they could see the awaiting disaster if we continued to blindly follow Marketing's impulses. Particularly one woman, Jane Gooden. She has enough character to fight costly changes to existing systems that only manipulated customers into thinking we had new products. She understands how the cumulative effect of quick changes eventually erodes stable systems. More important, she knew that resisting Marketing directly was pointless. We had to get ahead of them by developing and strengthening our respective staffs."

"You were organizing a coup?"

"I suppose you could say that, in a way. But it wasn't political, really, and I never got the chance. The merger with DexiaTel, smaller and less mature, with methods even more primitive than those of Celsus, quashed my plans."

Another pause to refill their beer glasses gives Megan a chance to peer into her old friend's brown eyes. How much is heat of the moment, and how much is baggage?

"Tell me Dustin, why didn't you leave if it was so bad?"

"Honestly, I don't know. Inertia? Or I suppose I held on to a delusion I'd always be able to change things once they fell apart completely. Even after Melange."

"Melange?" she says.

"Ancient history," he says, elliptically. He becomes silent, peers at her as if she's poking around in secret grounds, which she is, and then tenses up. She feels bad not letting him know she's aware of all this; however, she needs to hear it from Dustin firsthand.

"Come on Dustin. What's been going on?"

He finishes his glass and says nothing until the new pitcher comes. As he pours, he lets out a big sigh and tells her about the merger, about Melange, and about his subsequent isolation. Even though he's drinking his beer faster, the discussion seems to be sobering him up. It's a long story that takes several more pitchers—and a couple of coffees for Megan—to complete. At some point, Dustin seems to become unaware that he's speaking to anyone, let alone to Megan.

"So for all these months you've been doing nothing?" she says when he finishes, trying not to sound reproachful, or disappointed in him.

"That's right," he says, defiantly.

"I don't know what to say," she says.

"No wait. It's not like that. I told them I'd work on any assignment given me so it became Fortnum's choice to keep me idle."

"Really. Would you have given work to anyone who told you that?"

"Perhaps not. I don't care, actually. I just want to move on, both in life and in conversation. Like you, Megan. It's such a wonderful surprise to run into you. It's been so long that I haven't even heard what you're up to these days."

Megan hands him her business card and waits until he's read it, blushing slightly when his eyes widen in surprise.

"Vice President. You've done well."

"Several months after you left for Celsus, I took a management position with a small retail company, directing a large development group. Within a year, my entire IT department was outsourced. To a company called Paleo Transitions. They were small and relatively unknown. Actually, we still are. I certainly hadn't heard of them at the time. Maybe that's why I never saw the changes coming and why they came as such a surprise. Unlike my peers though, I didn't take it personally, nor did I resist. Instead, I investigated the reasons behind it and discovered they made sense. I took a political risk and openly and unapologetically supported the outsourcing."

"I'll bet that made you popular."

"Well, my efforts helped it succeed, but yes, it was at the cost of alienation from my colleagues, including the Vice President who had hired me. But my work and attitude impressed Paleo's owner, Jim Bradfield, enough to hire me away. A couple of years later, he promoted me to Vice President, Complex Solutions, at Paleo Transitions, the most senior role in the company. After him, of course."

"Very impressive," Dustin says.

His tone is sincere but Megan knows Dustin is not above envy and regret, especially while drinking. He'll wonder whether, under different circumstances, their positions might have switched. Perhaps they might have. However, she cannot quite imagine finding herself in his situation, let alone allowing it to go on for so long.

"So, what do you plan to do now?" she says.

"No plans. Take it easy for a while. The market's awful and since I got a decent severance there's no rush. Hell, I may even do something else."

"Outside of IT?"

"Fifteen years is long enough, don't you think? It's not interesting any more, especially with all those nerds who keep getting nerdier."

"Those so-called nerds look up to you and always will. They need people like you, as well, strong people. Your problem is that you were far too big a fish in far too small a pond." She leans forward, takes his hand between hers. "DexiaTel has diluted your imagination and ambition, but not killed it. Only you can do that. They can't handle you because they know you can easily handle them. It's time for you to realize that, unless they've killed your spirit too."

"Are you trying to tell me something?"

She smiles, one that is at the same time warm and stern.

"Come by my office tomorrow and meet my boss."

"One more pitcher?"

"Maybe it's time you got home, got some rest, Dustin."

0111

Megan is waiting for him inside the door of the medium-sized office building. A black-tiled open space leads to a wide, curving security desk and a large lobby. Elegant sofas and chairs that recline ensure visitors a pleasant wait. Each is equipped with outlets and other plugs to connect devices. Two people, dressed as salesmen and pointing at something on a laptop, glance up at him briefly but then return to their business. There is even a television and a working fireplace, the warmth of its flame strong enough to reach Dustin.

A security guard watches with cautious but friendly eyes as Dustin greets his old friend. She looks slightly older than she did in the bar, more mature in her expensive blue and white pantsuit; Dustin now wishes he'd worn a tie.

"Quite a waiting area," he says.

"More of an employee lounge, actually. Claude at reception is excellent at turning back salespeople and we prefer not to keep those we invite waiting. Those two you see over there, they work for us. Sometimes people just need a change of surroundings. The entire building belongs to Paleo, although we rent space to our clients. Let me show you around before we meet with James."

He follows her to the elevator—there is only one he can see but for some reason suspects there's a hidden one somewhere—and watches as she pushes and the number five button lights up. Seconds later, the doors open and lead out to a broad floor filled with small desks in what seems an organized pattern but of a shape Dustin cannot determine at ground level. A honeycomb? The absence of cubicle walls increases the brightness sweeping in through the windows.

"I should have brought sunglasses," he says, and Megan chuckles. "And where's the security door? Don't you have badges?"

"No badges, Dustin. We're still small enough to know each other. As far as security doors go, we do have them on the Paleo-only floors. This, however, is a customer retraining floor, and we leave it up to our customer to manage who comes and goes."

"Customer retraining? The way you say it, it sounds like brainwashing."

"Ha ha, funny."

"No, I didn't mean to criticize."

"You'd be surprised at how well things work if you leave everything open. We've never experienced an issue with theft of any kind. And all the desks have lockable drawers."

As they walk about the floor, Dustin is startled at the lack of privacy but impressed by the quietness, despite all the conversations taking place.

"Where are the meeting rooms?" he says.

"In a sense, it's all a meeting room," Megan says, her arms describing an arc.

She then explains the purpose of the floor is to show customers who want to break down the walls between IT and their business departments how to do it by putting the IT developers together with the people who use them.

"It's one thing to reorganize one's staff and remove the functional silos. But we've found the ergonomic component—in which the physical walls are removed—is equally as important, although usually harder to implement. So we host them until they can. You could compare it to a flight test simulator, although not as glamorous."

"Tthis is exactly what you and I were doing so long ago."

"Precisely. Only I've taken it much further here at Paleo and helped James transform his outsourcing firm into much more. Here we teach our methodology, if they don't have one, and adapt theirs if they do, in a controlled environment. They can then take this back to their organizations to implement on their sites. With our help, of course."

"They're doing actual work?"

"Oh yes, immersion is the proof in our pudding."

"I'm sure those organizations would be grateful."

"You'd think so, but of course, with all change, there are resisters. They remain back in their offices scrambling to find ways to undermine us. They're never successful but they can be disruptive."

"Yes," Dustin says, "I can imagine that type."

Megan leads him back to the elevator, which they take to the penthouse floor. She swipes her key chain at an invisible target, and a door slides open. They walk some distance to a large office with two rooms, one a meeting area and the other an office overlooking the highway, its door partly open.

"At last, a traditional office setting," Dustin says.

"Except no receptionist," Megan says.

She knocks at the door and they enter. A man with thin blond hair is sitting behind a long, oval-shaped desk with a glass top and metallic, triangular legs. As Megan introduces Dustin to James Bradfield, the man grasps Dustin's hand in a powerful handshake. He is tall, about six-foot-three, and sturdy as a tight end, exuding the confidence of a movie star.

"Megan has selected you for a specific role with a particular client of ours," he says. "Generally, I adopt her recommendations without question. However, this project is unique in many ways that you'll learn about, which is why I had to meet you in person first."

At Megan's prompting, Dustin gives Bradfield a concise, organized history of his career, editing out the alcohol-fuelled vitriol of the night before. To Dustin's relief, Bradfield shows no interest in the past months. His questions and interest focus primarily on Dustin's experience at DexiaTel around the time of the merger.

"Bring him along tomorrow," Bradfield says, to Megan, before excusing himself for another appointment.

Megan's nod irks Dustin and he finds it presumptuous of Bradfield to assume he will work for him just like that. And the way Bradfield is anxious for them to leave seems rude. She suggests they go for a coffee in the cafeteria, stopping first at Megan's office so she can get her briefcase.

"I bet it feels like we've blindsided you," Megan says, bringing a tray with coffee for Dustin and hot chocolate for her.

"That's an understatement," Dustin says. "I don't know anything about your company, let alone about this special role."

"Listen Dustin, although we may act like it, we are not taking it for granted that you will accept our offer. But I'm pretty sure you will."

"So, there's an offer?"

"Yes. Most definitely."

"But you won't tell me the details. Great. This is more convoluted than a project run by Chuck Bates."

Megan laughs, louder than Dustin thinks the remark deserves. Then something strikes him and he glares at her.

"You know who Chuck Bates is?"

Without hesitation, Megan shakes her head.

"I just assume he's one of your former colleagues. You probably mentioned him last night."

"Right. I don't think so."

"So what do you think of James?"

"He is impressive, I'll admit. A bit rude."

"Not at all—oh, you mean giving us the bum's rush. All right, I can reveal one thing, which you should find amusing."

"I'm listening."

"Jim is about to meet with someone you know."

"Who?"

"Someone you know quite well."

"Come on Megan, I'm getting tired of—"

"Clay Fortnum."

"What? Is he involved with this, whatever this oh-so-secret offer entails?"

"Relax Dustin. Actually, it's just a coincidence but it's why we had to get out of there—imagine the reaction if he'd seen you. I thought you'd find it funny but I suppose I was wrong."

"Just tell me Fortnum has nothing to do with this, project or whatever it is?"

Megan pauses, making no effort to hide her careful word selection.

"No, this project does not involve Clay Fortnum's participation."

"Then why are they meeting?"

"Why do you care? You don't work at DexiaTel any more."

Touché, Dustin thinks. He's out of a job and an old friend, someone he respects more than anyone, is ready to offer him something. And for that he cannot wait a day or two?

Megan pulls a stack of papers from her briefcase, hands him a contract, effective from that day, along with a non-disclosure document. When he sees the hourly rate on the offer, he smiles. For that amount, he would not only tolerate Fortnum, but also wash the man's car.

1000

Dustin's throat dries when he recognizes, in turn, Charles Wenham, Stu Cairns, and Miranda Fisher walking in to the

Paleo Transitions boardroom. The three executives barely acknowledge the former DexiaTel employee, only enough to show they are not as surprised to see him, as he is to see them. Is this a trick? A childish part of him considers getting up and leaving when Megan pats his arm and smiles reassuringly. While Bradfield shakes hands with the newcomers, Dustin looks out the door and into the hallway.

"Expecting to see someone else?" Bradfield says, to Dustin, before shutting the door.

Bradfield does not wait for a reply and guides the visitors to the seats closest to him, while Megan and Dustin sit at the other end of the table. Moments later, a man and a woman enter, Deepak and Cassandra. He'd only met them minutes earlier but at the time they looked familiar. Only now does he recall encountering them on a snowy day a few weeks earlier by the elevators at DexiaTel.

"It is my understanding introductions are not necessary," Bradfield says, with mock irony.

Dustin sighs. While happy to find work, and to reunite with his old friend, the idea of it involving DexiaTel seems distasteful. The aloofness of the DexiaTel executives is particularly unnerving. As if they want to maintain distance between themselves and their ex-employee. It gives Dustin the sense he is both an aid and a traitor.

Megan steps to the front and reviews progress to date. Her presentation is polished and professional; Dustin feels a genuine sense of pride for her. Now he grasps Paleo's role, which is part consultation for recruitment and reorganization and part outsourcing; combined, nothing short of an IT coup. He's dreamed so often of such a thing before. Yet the sceptic inside him remains doubtful.

A detailed discussion ensues, or rather a question and answer session, between Deepak, Cassandra, and primarily Stu Cairns on the DexiaTel side. It's a performance, not for Dustin, but for the other two executives. The more Stu speaks, the more Dustin's doubts recede. These executives really do intend an upheaval and are willing to accept the consequences. Or at least most of them.

"Now these two projects that belong to Joyce Morrison," Cassandra says, "since they're mostly outsourced, can continue—"

"Pardon me," Dustin says, drawing a wary glance from everyone but Megan, "but who is the outsourcer?"

"Ah, let me see," the woman says, leafing through a stack of sheets. "Yes, here it is, P&L Solutions, Incorporated—PALS?—anyway, apparently they do quite a bit of work for this manager."

"Yes they do," Dustin says, his voice rising, "and unless that stops, your plans will fail. You can't clean up anything without eliminating the parasites."

"That's absurd, they're just a vendor," Cassandra says.

"There's no one in this room more excited about what you intend to do," Dustin says. "However, the pain will be much harder than you think. The plan, as it stands, will likely work but not with lasting effect. There are plenty of deep-rooted elements I haven't seen addressed yet."

Dustin sits back down, ready for an onslaught of questions and challenges, but the room remains quiet for nearly a minute.

"Do you propose," Stu says, "to personally take responsibility for identifying and filling those gaps."

"Yes," Dustin says, without hesitation, without looking at his new employers.

Megan smiles at him in a way that makes him wonder if all this was orchestrated. Suddenly, everyone's at ease, even Deepak and Cassandra.

"That's all well and good," Miranda Fisher says, "but won't this mean retooling the plan?"

Bradfield walks over and puts his hands on Dustin's shoulders.

"On the contrary. With Mr. Freeman on board, we can accelerate the schedule. His insight and participation will shave weeks into days. And tonight I want to hold a little celebration, a christening if you will, of this voyage of ours."

In the small restaurant in a secluded corner of the main floor of the Paleo Transitions building, a private room has been arranged in luxurious fashion. The rectangular redwood table can seat eighteen but only six of the tall black leather backed chairs are set. When the three DexiaTel executives arrive, they greet Dustin in the same warm manner as they did Megan and Bradfield. The mood is formal but celebratory. Bradfield sits at one end of the table with Wenham at the other. Dustin is next to Megan who is on Bradfield's right,

Stu and Miranda across from them. In the center of the table, six opened bottles of dark red wine stand on guard. Tiny, square tables surround the room, showcasing antique urns and vases portraying scenes from Homer. Giant rectangular friezes engulf the two long walls, depicting more mythical images. Bradfield signals the waiters to pour.

"To change," he says, standing up, raising his glass.

Everyone stands to echo the toast. Then they sit for the first course. Before it arrives, Stu Cairns asks for attention.

"Jim, the three of us were talking on the way here. We agreed there is something that would help us out immensely, make us feel even more assured." He looks at Wenham and Fisher who both nod. "We are fine with Dustin's participation and trust he'll do what's needed. However, we do wonder how you can ensure his involvement does not cause more damage than good."

"I'm afraid I don't understand," Bradfield says.

"The thing is, the manner of his departure is still a concern for us."

"But we all agreed—"

"Just a moment, Megan," Bradfield says, and then addresses Wenham. "Charles, I hope we haven't all fallen under some kind of misunderstanding because, at least it seems to me, we are all here to initiate damage, in a sense."

Miranda Fisher chuckles sardonically but keeps silent while Wenham glances questioningly toward Cairns.

"Yes, yes," Cairns says. "You're right. But just to humour us, and particularly to humour me, there's something we'd like to ask of Dustin."

"Of course," Bradfield says. "What is it?"

"We'd like, I'd like, to hear from him, in his own uncensored words, how he came to be here. What were, or are, the circumstances at DexiaTel that brought this about? What's his view of the company and particularly the IT department? What's driving him?"

During months of idleness in his office, Dustin mentally scripted countless ways of relating his story. Never did he realistically think he'd one day face a receptive audience. But in this setting, and no longer employed by DexiaTel, he suddenly feels unprepared and lacking confidence in his ability to express those thoughts concisely and clearly.

"That's a rather vague request, Stu," Megan says, as if tracking Dustin's thoughts.

"It is, but I think there's a convenient way to do it," Cairns says, again glancing at the other two executives who nod.

"I'll do whatever I can," Dustin says.

Fisher smiles then with the amused but anxious anticipation of a voyeur realizing the show is much more than what she paid for. Wenham and Bradfield remain impassive while Megan watches like a big sister at a brother's recital. It is impossible to gauge the expression Cairns wears, as he has his wine glass held to his mouth. His lips twitch and it seems as if the man is suddenly unsure he wants to ask what he's about to ask. Then their eyes meet.

"Tell us about Melange," he says. "From start to end. Be candid and leave nothing out."

Dustin nods. He pauses to allow the servers to hand out the plates of salad. Then he then takes a drink of wine and clears his throat.

"Clay Fortnum announced the Melange project exactly two months after Celsus and DexiaTel merged, one month after his appointment as CIO. He showed up at my office, his face red, but wearing a good-buddy smile."

1001

"'Dustin,' he said, 'I want you to lead Melange.'

"'Sure thing,' I said. 'Given its priority and profile, I assume I'll get my pick of IT staff.'

"'Whoa, hold on there. We're a matrix organization now. Dedicated project teams and project personnel are outdated luxuries of the past. You'll have to negotiate resources with the development managers. Just like everyone else. That is, of course, once you've worked with them to establish cost estimates and procured funding. This project is going to be run by the books.'

"'I'm sure I'll manage most of it within my current team.'

"'You no longer have a current team. They've been reassigned amongst the development managers. New org charts have been drawn up. I'm making the announcements this afternoon.'

"'But I'm still a development director.'

"'There are no directors in my organization any more, remember. But fret not. This is not a demotion. Your pay isn't affected. Only your title has changed. You're now on Special Assignment and Melange is your one and only priority.'

"'But doesn't that make me dedicated project personnel then, an outdated luxury?'

"'Don't get smart. You know what I mean.'

"'Then what does Special Assignment mean, exactly?'

"'It means if the project is completed, satisfactorily, you'll be up for an extra bonus.'

"'Not that, the work.'

"'It's a prestigious assignment, one you're best suited for.'

"'Ah good, then my level is still superior to the other managers.'

"'I didn't say that. In fact, it's the other way around. You're going to have to follow their direction.'

"'How the hell do you expect that to work?'

"'It will work if you learn to adapt. You once told me how much you love challenges so this is right up your alley.'

"He had me. Consolidating the various ordering systems within DexiaTel, making them appear as one to internal users and customers and vendors was a monstrous undertaking, a terrific challenge, tailor-made for my ego, a chance to correct so many weaknesses within the company's systems.

"Like so many telecom IT departments, ours had grown too quickly. Narrowly focused tactical applications sprouted into existence all the time—at least two a year—each developed in isolation, each developed with its own rushed methodology or lack of one, each developed to fulfill an expedient, nearsighted purpose. No technical strategy or strategy of any kind. With the merger, the problem multiplied. A new, large customer, with a complex order, might have to navigate—with the aid of confused sales staff—up to two dozen systems before their service was fully up and running.

"Not only that, hardware platforms varied greatly yet few were reliable enough to handle their own segment, let alone our entire business. I was the only one in the department who could handle such a massive consolidation. And I wanted it. Even at the cost of losing my team.

"A talented group, each possessing a blend of technical abilities and personal professionalism that ensured good relations with the business. Under Fortnum's set of managers, the good ones would soon quit the company while the more naïve, promising ones would deteriorate to the mediocrity of their new managers. A harsh price to pay but I chose to pay it and the announcements were made that afternoon.

"The next day I discovered Fortnum neglected to inform me of a couple of details. The first was that Melange would be an overlay project. In other words, no projects would be cancelled or suspended to free up people. The other item was an immediate moratorium on hiring.

"Under these constraints, which my ego foolishly convinced me I could overcome, I assembled the IT managers and other senior staff in an impromptu kick-off session. Getting universal support as quickly as possible was key. I honestly didn't think it would be difficult either, considering Melange's high profile. The project's visibility would appeal to everyone's ambitions, if not their fears.

"When every single invitee showed up late, I took it as a bad omen. I was furious but had to appear patient. I described the project, individually and painstakingly specifying each area's impacts as I saw them. Blank faces tested my patience further but I carried on.

"'What's the budget?' Chuck Bates said, when I finished.

"'We don't have a budget yet,' I said. 'That's what I need your help to determine.'

"'I can't give you people unless there's a budget.'

"Others nodded agreement. I told them not to worry about the budget right now, that we had money available to do the initial work, and that I would get the rest once we determined the entire cost. This placated everyone except Joyce Morrison.

"'There must be an overall cost target?' she said.

"'The overall cost is what we determine it to be,' I said. Now faces lit up with interest and, knowing how their minds worked, I had to qualify my statement. 'This project is not an open ticket to fund extras. Nothing unessential or unrelated to Melange can be part of it.'

"Even though the meeting achieved my basic objectives—formally opening the project and getting the initial people I wanted assigned—I left with an ill feeling about the journey ahead of me.

"Things went better when I met with the developers. Most understood what I wanted and some were as eager as I was, substantial new development being so rare. Indeed, a buzz went through the meeting for the first hour. It subsided somewhat when every single one of them emphasized that since they were not dedicated to Melange, they needed managerial guidance to balance Melange's demands with their other obligations. A subsequent appeal to Fortnum to give me a dedicated team, even if I had to get all new people and hire from outside, fell on deaf ears.

"I drew up a crude estimate of cost and time, which was riddled with assumptions. But it was good enough for this early stage and set a baseline. Using that number, we applied a percentage to fund the next stage of detailed analysis, which would further refine the estimate.

"We were off and, while perhaps not running, at least strolling."

"One of Fortnum's earliest organizational moves was to hire a fellow, Jacques Chartrand, whose mandate was to revamp our internal processes and tailor them for the new matrix organization. For some reason Jacques and his staff, if he had any, worked—still works—out of a separate office in Montreal. My first encounter with this gaunt fellow and his flimsy handshake was on one of his rare excursions away from his desk when Fortnum brought him to my office. The two of them were smiling like used car salesmen.

"'Dustin, have you had a chance to review Jacques's work?'

"'A hundred pages of it or so, a thousand to go,' I said.

"'But you have them.'

"'Sure,' I said, pointing to the stack of four elegantly labelled blue binders at the end of my desk. 'Were you looking for feedback from me?'

"'Not exactly,' Fortnum said, then gave Jacques a sly look that made me uneasy. 'You see, we're looking for a real life project, a meaty one, to fine-tune Jacques's work. Thus, we're instituting these processes for Melange, immediately.'

"Again I kept quiet, because I was stunned. My silence seemed to encourage Clay and give Jacques confidence.

"'With the rigour and control we can achieve by engaging these processes with our business partners,' Fortnum said, 'we will ensure the project progresses accordingly to meet our IT and corporate goals.'

"I wondered what he meant by accordingly and looked at Jacques to see if he was bewildered by this too; the acolyte, however, was too busy writing down every word Fortnum uttered.

"'I don't agree,' I said. 'Based on what I've read, these processes are only partially developed and of no value yet, especially not for a complex project like Melange.'

"As I spoke, Fortnum kept shaking his head. 'I'm afraid you have no choice in the matter,' he said. 'I've already told our business and IT stakeholders. The other managers support them one hundred percent.'

"'Oh? I can just imagine how Jane Gooden and Stu Cairns responded.'

"'You're right, it won't be an easy sell to everyone. People have difficulty with change, I suppose—'

"'You mean they don't know?'

"'That's the other reason we're here. They know in a general sense, they know it's coming, just not the specifics. I felt it best to let you conduct a Q&A session with them at your next project meeting.'

"Too late I realized this was just the little ambush setting me up for a bigger one. Fighting it didn't seem worth the trouble, though. That could slow me down much more than giving in would, I rationalized. At least this way I'd be able to put my own spin on the content.

"'And be assured that Jacques will be available as much as you need. After all, Melange is the pilot project for his efforts now, his beta test, if you will.'

"'Is that so?' I said, looking at the Quebecer. 'You'll make yourself available?'

"'Yes, of course,' he said.

"'Perfect, Jacques, then I'll let you conduct the Q&A?'

"'Oh, no, no, I am not as familiar with the project as you are with these processes. Besides, I am needed in Montreal then so it's not possible for me to attend in person. But I will conference in.'

"His presentation slides came the next day. Dull yet colourful, they depicted a bureaucratic treasure trove of request forms, signoff forms, authorizations, charters, logs, risk plans, and other documents. A constant theme or principle ran clearly through it all though, plenty of paperwork for Jane's people, but minimal interaction between them and the developers.

"Unlike when Jane and I worked together before, when my staff would work closely with her people to determine the solution, to establish which processes would remain human and which would be automated, and then figure out the business rules within each, it was now up to her team to do all that. IT's responsibility—aside from actually building whatever survived all that—was to approve, accept or reject, with little guidance or objectivity provided as to the criteria to make such determinations.

"I'm only the messenger, I kept telling myself, as I somehow fumbled my way through the session. It helped to have a sympathetic audience who probably understood I was as much a victim as they were. Not too much damage occurred until Jacques, blind to the body language, decided to summarize.

"'. . . and so by rigorously engaging and controlling these processes, we will accordingly achieve progress on this project, and all future ones . . .'

"The mood in the room plunged. Everyone's eyes turned from the little speaker on the desk to me.

"'Any questions?' came from the phone.

"'Sure, I have a question,' Jane Gooden said, staring at me. 'What is this garbage?' She looked genuinely hurt, betrayed. Not only was Jane my counterpart on the business side, she was a friend, someone I had worked extremely well with for years. Now I understood Fortnum's insistence I present this, while the 44477culprit hid behind the telephone.

"'I'm sorry you feel that way,' Jacques said. 'I feel these new processes, given time, will work out very well.'

"'Of course you would, Jacques,' Jane said. 'It's a fine little industry you're creating for yourself while also making sure your work is done by us.'

"'It's called business ownership,' Jacques said, with some force. 'These processes attach responsibility to the owners. By having you document your requirements in depth, before IT gets involved, we make sure they are accurate so we can save time, save money.'

"'You know this is going to delay the project,' Jane said, to me.

"'I don't disagree,' I said. 'Take it up with Stu Cairns.'

"'You can count on that, Dustin.'

"Influential as Stu was, I knew Jane would not win her battle and I think she knew as well. I was right.

"Subsequently, tensions on the project ran high, not only between IT and Jane's team, but also internally, within IT, as we struggled with the new procedures. Yet while Jacques's documentation system was stifling in so many ways, its lack of thoroughness became its downfall. People quickly found loopholes and gaps. It didn't take long for cracks to appear in Jacques's masterpiece like decals on a cheap t-shirt.

"In the end, we didn't lose too much time and we formulated an architectural design of how the new system would appear to those using it, as well as how it would integrate with our internal systems."

"Chartrand's forms and processes were kid's play compared to the architects. Fortnum had recently hired three technical gurus to define and implement a corporate IT strategy for DexiaTel. The company needed one.

"Years before.

"It was too late now. Before dreaming up how things could be in the future, the IT department had to clean things up, Melange being a giant first leap.

"Similar to Jacques and his red-tape workshop, these so-called architects worked in isolation, making little effort to interact with those who would have to live with the product of their efforts. Outside the company, though, they were very sociable. Few vendor information sessions and conferences passed by that they did not find the time to attend. Subscribing to all those technical magazines ensured they didn't miss a single item of technical interest in the general IT world.

"Coincidentally—or not, as I was getting more paranoid about such things—the day before we finalized our project architecture, they published a utopian diagram of how DexiaTel's computer systems were to look in the future. They even took the trouble to arrange a special meeting to present it to me.

"I remarked it was a pretty picture that must have taken hours to make readable on one page. Ted Scholes smiled and took it as a compliment at first. The other two, Al Chang and Fred Holochuk, were content to remain quiet and stoic, like Secret Service men.

"'So when's it all going to happen?'

"'We cannot speak in terms of dates,' Ted Scholes said. 'This is a journey measured by achievement, not time.'

"'Well, I appreciate you taking the time to show this achievement to me but I have to get back to Melange."

"'We didn't come here to consult you, or get your opinion,' Scholes said. 'This has to do with Melange.'

"'What could this possibly have to do with my project?'

"'We have studied your designs. As you can probably determine from the picture, there are certain elements of Melange that clash with our strategy.'

"'Are you saying my design is unworkable?' I said.

"'It is not a question of the workability of your design. It is a question of future fit.'

"'I don't understand,' I said, although I understood perfectly and just wanted to put them on the spot.

"'Your design needs to change in order to complement our strategy,' Ted said, getting to the point quicker than he usually did.

"'That would mean a lot of rework, not to mention probably another, say, two million dollars for new software and hardware.'

"'Money we would spend eventually, anyway,' Ted said.

"'I get it now,' I said. 'You have no money so you're trying to piggyback on my budget.'

"This appeared to offend all three, which was fine because they were only catching up to how I felt. My irritation increased when I asked them how they would advise I handle the inevitable delays and they said nothing, their looks intimating that was not their problem.

"'Guys,' I said. 'I'm all for architectural strategy and future planning but not at the expense of tactical operational projects. Melange is essential to the company, now. It can't wait for some pie-in-the-sky architecture that will become obsolete next month. In fact, I'd go as far as to declare that, without Melange, there will be no company to use your architecture.'

"'Oh don't be so dramatic, Dustin,' Scholes said. 'It'd be a waste to do it one way now, and then redo it later.'

"'Why would we have to redo it later? Why not just change your diagram?'

"Three heads bobbled and looked at me as if I had blasphemed. Once again, Ted was the first to recover.

"'Impossible. This is the architecture. This is the future.'

"'You mean it can't change?'

"'No, it can't. We've already gotten Clay's approval.'

"'We're talking technology here,' I said. 'Things change. Do we really want to tie ourselves down so rigidly?'

"'Are you questioning our expertise? This strategy has come from a lot of research.'

"Bull, I thought. It all came from brochures, vendor demonstrations, slick sales people, and their own Lego-inspired imaginations. I was tempted to go through their diagram, highlight every box, circle, line, arrow, and challenge them to come up with a living example where they had seen it implemented, and working, hell, even a place where someone had committed any money or effort.

"But I was getting tired of their parochial attitude and the temptation to give in, to let the chips fall where they may, and to let Fortnum and Cairns battle it out crossed my mind. I couldn't do that because I cared too much about my project now, and I was still smarting from my failure with Chartrand. I chose a quicker escape.

"'I'm afraid, fellows,' I said, 'this discussion is too late. We're too far along with our design, and we can't turn back.

"'Of course you can,' Chang said.

"'You haven't gotten our sign-off,' Holochuk said.

"'We sign-off all project designs,' Scholes said.

"They looked panicked, as if given a sudden glimpse of their real value.

"'Yes, under the previous processes that would be true. But, and trust me I've checked this out thoroughly, it appears Jacques hasn't completed that part of the architectural approval process yet. Check it out for yourself. In Book Three, it's on pages 62, 88, and 191. In Book Five, there are a several paragraphs on page 471—'

"'All right, all right,' Scholes said.

"'So, in accordance with those processes, which Clay ordered us to follow to the nth degree, I'm not even allowed to request your approval. Therefore, as far as I'm concerned, ipso facto, my architecture is automatically approved.'

"I walked out the room, whistling down the hallway to drown out the confused muttering and empty escalation threats."

1010

"That peril averted, each of the development areas could now refine and solidify their technical approaches and functional designs for a solid cost estimate. I held a session to review the numbers, validate the assumptions, and identify gaps and duplications. I decided to invite the managers too because they would have come anyway.

"We found little duplication but plenty of gaps, a clear sign of how little discussion had taken place between groups on overlapping items; without exception each assumed the other would cover it. A full week of daylong debates about lines of responsibility took place. By the end of that week, the cost had ballooned to twice the revised amount, which itself was double the original estimate.

"'We've shaved our costs down as much as possible,' Joyce Morrison said, supposedly speaking for everyone after I challenged them.

"'Is that so?' I said, and then leafed through some pages until I found her team's contribution. 'I see here you have Todd, Ibrahim, and Sarah budgeted for full time on the project. Are you saying I will have them full time?'

"'It's too early to work out the detailed work assignments of my entire team. I have other projects to consider too. This is just to make sure we're covered.'

"'Listen, Joyce, I'll make you a deal. If you commit these three full-time to Melange, then I'll have no problem taking your estimate forward.'

"'You know I can't do that.' Joyce Morrison said.

"'I don't know that. But if your staff commitment can't match your budget needs, it stands to reason something must be cut.'

"'Why be so black and white about it?' she said.

"'Even if we were to go back and refine estimates, we can't because you've run out of seed money,' Chuck said.

"'Yeah, I'd hate to have to pull my staff to work on other projects because this one's run out of funds already,' Joyce Morrison said.

"'You can't afford that kind of disruption, Dustin,' Joyce Blanton said, flashing her lovely but phoney smile.

"'You have to go forward with these figures,' Chuck said.

"No one would budge and, considering my lack of authority, I had no recourse. Ridiculous as I thought they were, the estimates didn't reflect on me. To my surprise, there was no serious protest from the steering committee, although I did spot many raised eyebrows. The funds were approved in less than an hour. I felt my first tinge of optimism since before I'd heard the name, Clay Fortnum.

"Two weeks later Chuck and Joyce Morrison came to see me. While Joyce inspected her nails, Chuck was fidgety.

"'Come on, Chuck, just tell him,' Joyce said.

"'Yeah, listen Dustin, in reviewing our estimates with Al and Fred, it seems we missed something for the Order Transport interface between two of our systems.'

"'I see. How much?'

"'Excuse me?'

"'How much is this going to cost?'

"The amount Chuck quoted was nearly ten percent of the new budget, and I assumed he was low-balling. Joyce offered a look of sympathetic resignation. 'No use getting upset, nothing can be done about it,' she said. 'We need that interface so be a good boy and get the extra money.'

"'So what do we take out?' I said.

"'What do you mean?' Chuck said.

"'What I mean is that if I go back for more money, after we've already quadrupled our original estimate, I'll get my ass kicked.'

"They looked at me as if I was speaking Greek to them. Chuck argued that everything was essential and nothing could be removed. We went back and forth on this for a while until once again I faced my Achilles heel, my powerlessness.

"There was a steering committee meeting the next day, which Stu always attended. Clay Fortnum, for some reason, probably instinctual, skipped this one. Good thing for him he did. My clients reacted like a native tribe drawing their bows after a perceived insult to their chief when I said:

"'There is a crucial interface, that we missed, and—'

"'If it was crucial then how could it have been missed?'

"'That's something I'll get to the bottom of, but for now we need to address the immediate impacts.'

"'Speaking of impacts, how much more work does this mean for my team?'

"'It's an internal interface. It doesn't affect how the system looks or operates, to the end-user. From your standpoint it's only a cost issue.'

"Fortunately there was enough goodwill still remaining between Jane and myself that she did not belabour this point. However, she did comment on the rising cost of the project, predicting this was only the beginning.

"'No it's not, it's the end,' Stu said, his first words of the meeting. 'Because you need to find a way to cover it with the money you already have. You are not getting any more money, or time. I don't want to hear about this, or any other problem, again. You have money—a lot of money—and if you can't manage this project within that amount then . . .'

"And he went on for another full minute. It wasn't pleasant but I was glad this discovery had occurred when it had, not later. Between the padded estimates and my own creativity, I'd find a way. That was as long as Jane's suspicion that this was just the start didn't come true."

"The experience did force me, at the expense of other duties, to pay closer attention to the budget. One day I noticed purchase orders for a vendor whose name I didn't recognize. As the development managers could procure work on my project, without informing me beforehand, this was not unusual. And if the purchaser had been anyone other than Joyce Morrison, I might have let it slide.

"When I explained this purchase order would put her over her group's portion of the budget, Joyce shrugged, as if it was a trivial concern. She then revealed that the PO would cover all the rest of her development work, including some of her other estimates.

"'It's still too much,' I said. 'Who's the vendor? Give me their number and I'll negotiate a better price.'

"She shook her head, told me not to bother. She made a phone call and within a minute two guys in jeans and golf shirts showed up. Perry Heller and Larry Steen. They smiled nervously, probably sensing I wasn't happy to see them.

"'So you're P&L Solutions, Incorporated?' I said.

"They nodded.

"'PALS, that's cute. So, the last time I saw you guys, was, let me remember, oh yeah, when I shipped you out during the contractor purge. Isn't that right?'

"Perry and Larry used to be our go-to guys on several key systems for years before the merger. There was so much work for them they had offices onsite. As self-incorporated contractors, they handled their own taxes, expense deductions, income deferrals, et cetera. Yet in all other ways—their own desks, telephones, nameplates, and even computers—they were like full-time staff. They'd even developed that complacent sense of entitlement one finds in long-time employees. However, if the government ever classified them as employees—something the tax people were threatening to do—we would have been in trouble. We would have been on the hook to withhold income tax from the date the government declared them employees. Years of income tax. Every team in the department would have been affected, a potential exposure of millions of dollars. Hence the purge.

"All directors and managers were mandated to eliminate long-term contracts, either by hiring them full-time—an unappealing solution to most of them—or by not renewing their contracts. While this distressed most managers in the department, I saw it as a great opportunity to rid ourselves of these crutches. Perry and Larry, touted as elite developers, had developed a reputation for solving problems quickly. They were quick, but what people didn't see, especially managers without technical backgrounds, like Joyce Morrison, was that their programming abilities were average.

"With no one looking over their shoulders, they'd developed bad habits such as skipping documentation and implementing hasty designs that obfuscated and complicated future changes. Their sloppiness created booby traps, landmines for which they only had the map. No one could guess how much of what we were paying them went to enhancing our systems and how much to fix problems of their making. Our programmers grew so intimidated by their indecipherable code that none dared touch it. Our dependence on them grew, not because of their skills, but because of their specific, proprietary knowledge of their own bad work. Worst of all, as virtually all projects touched upon the functions they supported, bottlenecks occurred when we had more work than they could handle.

"The only way out was to go cold turkey, to suffer the pain of fixing the damage, and that's why I had welcomed the purge. That they were back, in a new incarnation, explained a lot, not the least of which was how the budget had gotten so high.

"'Does Clay know they're still doing work for us?' I said, to Joyce.

"'Actually, we've never stopped,' Perry said.

"Joyce glared at him before answering. 'Yes, Clay knows, just as he knows we need their skills, their experience and expertise.'

"'You guys,' I said, 'Joyce and I need to talk. Why don't you get back to work and we'll be in touch to review your estimates.'

"They left and I explained to Joyce that we had not budgeted to use vendors this much, that most of our estimates were based on cheaper in-house labour. I wanted them off the project immediately. She argued it was too late. Sadly, I had to admit she was right. I asked her to reduce their estimates, or rates, or both and was a little surprised when she said she'd try. She was in a strange mood, less fiery than usual, although still defensive.

"'I'm just curious, have you been using these two all this time since I booted them out?'

"'Sure,' Joyce said.

"'We were all supposed to eliminate our use of contractors several years ago.'

"'They're not contractors. They are a vendor now.'

"'I see. So they have other clients too?'

"'How the hell would I know?'

"'It seems to me that incorporating as a company is a tactic, a thin cover, especially if their only customer is DexiaTel. I think we're still exposed from a taxation standpoint.'

"'Whatever. Not my problem. Not yours either. We need them because of all the urgent projects, especially Melange.'

"I could never put a name to it but, underneath Joyce's general complacence, there seemed to be a deep layer of bitterness, as if there was someone capable imprisoned behind the comfort of bureaucracy. It was this person I was trying to reach when I said:

"'No, you still need them because you're too lazy to develop your own people to replace them.'

"Her eyes flared, her mouth twitched, and the confrontational Joyce I knew returned in full force.

"'Look, buddy, you try finding capable legacy coders out there. They don't exist. They don't teach those old computer languages any more. You have to pay for this talent.'

"'Talent? You actually think these guys are good?'

"'Of course. There's nobody who can work as fast as they can. And their stuff works.'

"'Joyce, I've seen their work. It's mediocre, at best. They're lazy, they cut corners and hardcode all the time.'

"'Not true. You don't know what you're talking about.'

"'Have you ever personally looked at their programs? Do you even know what hardcoding means?'

"'I'm not a programmer. It's not my job.'

"'Precisely, Joyce, all the more reason to get an independent audit from someone who is or was.'

"'They're the best I have and they're doing my development for Melange. End of story. Besides, it's not your problem any more, is it?'

"Then she adopted a blank stare, that facial wall, polite, even friendly, yet impenetrable, a common expression amongst Fortnum's managers since his reign began. Even if she would ever give credence to what I had to say, she would never be intelligent enough to understand it. Joyce Morrison, the quintessential Fortnum manager."

"By now my budget had eroded so much we had no choice but to cut items. It took a great deal of creativity and much negotiating with Jane and her team but we somehow managed to do it. Even more surprising was Jane's reasonableness about it. She was having resource troubles too so I think our reduced scope came as a relief to her. The less we built, the less she'd have to test and train; and it would be all IT's fault, my fault.

"I got us back on a plan, within our budget and, now probably most important, within our original timelines. However, not being immune to Murphy's Law, I was not surprised to receive another visit from Chuck. He hesitated before putting on a strangely triumphant smile.

"'I have good news for you, Dustin. From speaking with Joyce, I know how you feel about using vendors.'

"I stifled a groan. Whenever Fortnum's people prefaced 'good news' by paraphrasing my words, it was bound to be bad news for me.

"'I've been able to free up Missy Patenkoffel to lead the development work for my area.'

"I couldn't have imagined anything worse. I was unable to decide whether to come up with logical arguments to fight this or to wonder how I hadn't seen this coming.

"'She can begin next week,' he went on. 'Her other obligations should wind down over the next two to three weeks. Then she'll be dedicated to Melange, full time. Who knows, with that much firepower, she might be able to assist in other areas of the project as well. I've already spoken to a couple of other managers about this.'

"'Chuck, that woman is not working on Melange,' I said.

"'Hey, I'm just trying to help the cause. She has the two qualities you've been bugging us for all along, full time availability, and cheap internal labour.'

"'You forgot to mention she's a cancer on any project.'

"His shocked reaction almost made me laugh; he actually seemed hurt.

"'Well, I want her to work on Melange, and it's my call.'

"'That's true, technically.'

"'What do you mean, technically?'

"'Chuck, I'll take her on under one condition.'

"'Good, sure. What condition?'

"'That at the end of the project I conduct her performance review.'

"'I can't do that.'

"'Why not?'

"'Why not? I'm her manager. It's my responsibility to do her review. I'll come to you for feedback, sure, but I'm the one who compiles her overall score.'

"'But one hundred percent of it will come from Melange, assuming she's truly available full time. Or are you saying you'll be giving her other assignments?'

"'Don't put words in my mouth. She's all yours. It's just that, what you're asking for, well, that's not the process. That's not how matrix management works.'

"'So change the process, just this time. What are you scared of?'

"'I don't think I have the—no, it would set a bad precedent. Besides, she wouldn't go for it.'

"'Why wouldn't she? It's a high profile project, a great opportunity for positive recognition.'

"I almost had him then but Clay happened to walk by. For no apparent reason, maybe an instinctive nurturing sense that a sycophant was in trouble, the CIO poked his head in the door. Bolstered by his idol's presence, Chuck returned to his original stance. So now, on top of everything else, I got Missy.

"The busybody was surprisingly co-operative at first, pleasant even. But I wasn't fooled. Sure enough, after a series of meetings, especially with Jane's group, but also some within IT, complaints began to stream in. Not surprisingly, most had to do with the Issues Log.

"My first glance at this vile document told me my worst fears had materialized. Overnight, she had logged twenty-four issues, each requiring meetings, escalations, updates. Most were existing work items so, in essence, her Issues Log had hijacked my project plan. The sad thing was that, because of Fortnum's matrix, I couldn't do much outside of complaining. But I was complaining so frequently then that any more would come out as whining. So I tried to train the team to recognize, and ignore, Missy's red herrings. But, like rats, they kept following the pied piping perfectionist.

"For masochistic amusement, I monitored one issue in particular, one I don't believe ever closed. It was about whether or not to design order entry screens to support Cyrillic script. I'd never heard of such a thing for a Canadian, or any English speaking, company. Missy explained it was in case we ever marketed directly to Eastern Europeans who couldn't, or didn't want to, transact with us in English or French. Huh?

"Every week I winced at the five, fifteen and once even a full thirty minutes that was wasted discussing this item and others like it. After the project, I discovered Jane had authorized, instructed, and even demanded Missy close the issue on five separate occasions. Each time Missy unearthed some obscure scenario to investigate and rule out, keeping the issue alive.

"Control is essential in running a project; I no longer had it. Perhaps I never had. I began to wonder whether all this stemmed from me; perhaps there was some fault in my perception putting me out of touch with reality. That I was out of touch with my department was a given. Fortnum's world was a reality I would never grasp. I felt isolated against virtually everyone else, at least within IT. Was my stubbornness blinding me to the truth?

"Even though we were at a crucial point, it seemed necessary to get away, to invest a few days to recalibrate myself and sort things out. Maybe I'd surrender and admit defeat after that."

<h2 style="text-align:center">1011</h2>

"Once away I faced a new challenge: resisting the temptation to stay away forever. An idle fear because an unfinished Melange would haunt me.

"But why is it only bad things should haunt you? Good things ought to do the same, no? And I had had many good IT experiences, many successes in the past. Why not look there for inspiration. Eagerly, I searched my house for old address books and business cards.

"The easiest to get hold of was Raj Perander, a senior analyst from the team Fortnum disbanded when he assigned me Melange. Only days after his transfer to Chuck Bates's group, Raj resigned. I never found out the true reason he left, as there was no going away party for him. I had assumed it was due to the change.

"I met him in a coffee shop, bought him an espresso, and discovered he had left IT altogether, taking time from his career to write a novel. He was reluctant to revisit the negativity of DexiaTel, but I persisted. He laughed sardonically when I told him about Missy.

"'Sorry, but you had to have seen that coming,' he said.

"'Did you? Is she a reason why you left?'

"'She drove me as nuts as she does everyone, but people like her are no reason to quit. Neither is Chuck. Nor Joyce Morrison, the architects, and so on. Believe it or not, I left for my own reasons, and was already contemplating a new path for my life. From what you describe though, I picked a good time.'

"I asked him to give me his take on the project, as he had worked on many of its impacted components before. He thought about it for a few seconds before answering.

"'You'll be there to see the end of it, although it will probably finish not as you, or anyone, expects. And through it all, you'll have to continue suffering with that pedantic little analyst and others like her. Once hooked on to big projects like this, people like her don't easily let go. And if you try to distract her with other work, she'll only mix it in with the rest. She's the embodiment of busywork.'

"'That's comforting,' I said.

"'That's not the worst of it. You can't appeal to others for help either. Her type is useful to the managers, not for her development skills, but rather her political possibilities. Missy is well aware of their high regard for her too, although blind to the distinction.'

"While not a heartening discussion, it helped to hear my perspective validated by someone I respected. I felt I was on the right track. At home, there was a message from Gerry Michaels, my first IT boss. Unfortunately, there was no time to call him back right away.

"My next appointment was with Archie Phelps, my CIO at the time of the merger, the man Fortnum replaced. Archie is the only superior I ever considered a role model. It had been sad for me to see him leave, especially to make way for someone like Fortnum, but Archie had done well for himself. He now ran a consulting business and kept in touch with people at DexiaTel, including some working on Melange. He grasped my situation right away.

"'You see the impending disaster, you see the project crashing and burning, and you're looking for ways to avert it. But because no one else can see it, or is willing to see it, you're helpless. Just bear in mind that the situation is not as bleak as you think right now and there's a good chance you'll discover a way to the end.'

"'You really think so?'

"He smiled at my sarcasm but then became serious. 'Before then, you'll experience many more difficulties. I heard about that little trick you pulled on Fortnum's architects, using his brand new processes against them. That will have pissed him off more than he'd ever show. You see, the architects are not only his pride and joy, but also his meal ticket. You made them, and by extension Fortnum, look like idiots.'

"'Then they look like what they are,' I said.

"'Be that as it may, Fortnum's out to make life difficult for you and his subordinates are only too willing to help. See how they emulate his behaviour, his looks, his tone, his words, his tactics. Believe me, whenever your name comes up, they're paying attention. It's in your interest to continue on and, as hard as it will be, contain your pride. Don't offend Fortnum any more. Regardless of how the project turns out, don't say or do anything to embarrass him. It'll only backfire.'

"'And if he provokes me?'

"'Take the high road, turn away, keep your dignity. Your views don't matter and your cleverness is irrelevant, because he has the power.'

"Difficult words to digest although I knew it was important for me to hear them.

"'One more thing, Dustin. Even with those precautions, this project will be your undoing in the department. You're already an outcast verging on becoming a pariah and will be one as long as Fortnum is in charge.'

"I was somewhat depressed when I called Gerry Michaels back. Our talk partially restored my spirits as we shared old anecdotes. About my current concerns, he had little to say beyond how things had changed for the worse since his day. 'No one wants to take the time to do things right these days,' he said. 'No wonder these old systems will never get replaced.' But he was able to provide current contact information for a list of names of people I remembered well, people I had not talked to for years. Most had moved on to different companies, some had even formed their own.

"Neil, a business analyst, talked about the unique nature of his role:

"'As the bridge between IT and the business, I bring together two groups that, regardless of overt niceties, and often in spite of them, do not want to talk each other, let alone work together. To think it can be otherwise is delusional. What I can do is insulate each side by trying to understand and respect their particular needs and circumstances, in their terms. I convince everyone their voices are heard during development and prove it during testing.

"'My approach contrasts those business analysts who play one side against the other and nurture the animosity, whether out of a basic weakness of character or simple laziness. They seek out and exploit each side's vulnerabilities, and then position themselves in the middle, blameless and free of responsibility when things deteriorate. There's always some undone or poorly done task, some failing that can be exposed, magnified, and blamed on someone. You can spot this type of business analyst easily because they tend to be loud and bombastic, using a powerful personality to disguise an impotent developer.

"'Perhaps worse, though, are the self-effacing ones who merely act as stenographers and messengers. They listen to the business and transcribe what they find to IT, verbatim, and likewise take what IT says to the business. There is no attempt at correlating or reconciling the inevitable contradictions. When the misunderstandings and blaming begins—and they invariably do—they retract their heads like turtles and hope for the best while the two sides fight it out.'

"Martin, still a systems analyst, chose to be philosophic:

"'For whom does a company invest in computer systems? For the people who will use them day in and day out? Or for the system developers? Obviously, for those who use them. But do the developers understand that? Do they care? Some do. Many don't. Always look behind what the developers say because they can be quite clever in explaining why something is not possible to do. They rely on excuses such as, "things have always been done this way; it's too difficult to change it in such and such time; we this and we that." When these phrases are common, you don't have developers but IT janitors, expensive, lazy, and insecure janitors.'

"Justin, a systems architect, offered his own question:

"'What the hell would a dysfunctional IT department like yours need with an architect, let alone three? You guys need an architect as much as a homeless person needs an interior decorator.'

"Val, the best computer programmer I've ever worked with, pointed out the risk of specialists, those developers who only work on one system or one project, a situation tolerated, and even encouraged, at DexiaTel:

"'A co-dependency develops,' he said. 'The developer's value lies more in his knowledge of that system than in the skill of his craft. Managers seeking a quick exit from project jams, and to appease or impress superiors, overuse the expert, acknowledging the dependency, vowing to eliminate it next time. But the jams never end. The programmer gains leverage once he becomes, or is believed to have become, impossible to replace. And the programmer is stuck as well, attached to the security, addicted to the accolades. All his self-confidence and self-worth is invested in this narrow niche. He can't risk another taking his place, in case someone discovers his role is not as complicated as he's pretended. He willingly works all the overtime necessary, foregoing vacations and training, thus tying him to the special skills and knowledge required for that role. Depending on his personality, and that of his manager, you either wind up with a pathetic parasite, or an insufferable prima donna.'

"Karl, a former contract programmer, almost as talented as Val, echoed those comments about specialists, adding another aspect:

"'The situation worsens when the programmers are not employees. Any consultant who stays at the same place for a long time is an insecure leech. As his technical skills deteriorate, his survival instincts improve and he becomes a fixture. But you can't blame the consultant; the temptation's too strong. They get the security benefits of an employee along with the remuneration of a contractor. I certainly respect them above any manager who permits such situations to evolve.'

"None of this came as a revelation to me and everything these people had described to that point applied directly to DexiaTel. I'd become blind to it, perhaps wilfully so. All of my old friends and colleagues were kind enough not to ask what kept me at DexiaTel, although I was sure several wondered. I didn't want to hear any more but had to continue and face it all.

"Allan, a project manager, pulled no punches:

"'Your crisis with this Melange project is beyond any experience I've had. All organizations have similar problems but rarely so concentrated. A project can't succeed with so many stakeholders in control; matrix structures just don't work. I never take on a project unless I get complete control of every team member assigned. Ideally, I do the recruitment too but that's not normally possible any more so I don't mind compromising there. In those cases, though, I insist on doing performance appraisals of those assigned. You have to have leverage.'

"Terri, a development manager, laughed, rather unmercifully, throughout my Melange description before commenting:

"'Sorry Dustin, I don't mean to be unsympathetic. Keep in mind your problem is not this Missy character. In the end, she is inconsequential, forgettable, disposable. The real problem is the culture that creates Missy and others like her, and what keeps her kind around, and prospering. Your peers know exactly what she is, the effect she has, although some may not be consciously aware of it. They tolerate it because either they're too weak to resist her or they actually wish for projects to fail. If you lose those managers, you lose the Missy problem.'

"'A nice wish, but unrealistic,' I said.

"'That's right. Hence, her type will always be around. But they can be productive under certain circumstances. The managers who elevate that type of worker, the ones who promote such analytical recklessness and let such egos flourish, are the ones who create the monster. Haven't you read Frankenstein?'

"I told Gil, a director, about Terri's comments. He concurred and added:

"'You also have to dig deeper. Those managers may create and nourish the monster but someone else created the creators. In that respect, Terri gives your managers too much credit. I doubt they're bright enough to do this purposely, although they might be instinctively clever enough to profit from it. They know enough not to ask why, and to find their own advantage, and adapt.

"'But there is something much more dangerous behind people like Missy. It's a subtle but pervasive thing. You say the developers never stand up to her, but often complain about her, behind her back. This shows your developers are either ineffective or conniving, hazardous by-products of managers who hire and develop weak people.

"'And what makes them hire such people is their instinctual awareness of their own abilities. Behind their bravado, they realize their true value and will not hire anyone who can match or, heaven forbid, exceed that value. Thus, you can discover anyone's opinion of their self-worth by the people they hire. In those rare cases when they inadvertently hire someone strong and capable, or inherit one, watch out, for then they will turn vicious and reveal their true character. They'll attack that employee's self-esteem, micromanage them, take other steps to inhibit his or her growth. Why? In hopes of ultimately bringing that employee down to their level, or lower. Only those with a strong enough fortitude to recognize this can get away or survive. The rest, sadly, will find their careers slowly disintegrating.'

"Feargal, a consultant, listened sympathetically, before reaching into his jacket pocket:

"'Dustin, this matrix organization is a consultant's dream, a veritable cash cow. Please, do me a favour and take my card, take several in fact, and pass them around.'"

1100

"Not until the night before going back to DexiaTel did I realize that not a single one of my old friends and colleagues had offered me an escape. No one said, "Hey Dustin, why don't you give me your resume." Nor had I asked. Still, I went to sleep, my mind full of resolve, but my spirit woke full of dread, the latter borne out by what I discovered.

"Everything had become meetings. People who should have been coding what they had designed, and then testing what they had coded, were spending most of their day in conference rooms like traffic ticket fighters in a courtroom, listening to cases having nothing to do with them while waiting for theirs to come up.

"It would have been naïve of me to hope for no new issues, but I had never expected the number to triple. Most were new but plenty had re-opened; together they far outnumbered those closed. The last of the programming was due within a month, although we still had three months worth left to complete. Not only that, we could barely pay for two weeks of development before encroaching on the testing and implementation budget. Melange was a certifiable disaster.

"Missy was no less annoying yet it all seemed to have overwhelmed her, humbled her. I took advantage of this and asked her to compile a synopsis of the situation. Her analysis was succinct, her document surprisingly clear. She was even on time for our meeting to discuss it.

"'This shows how much work we have to do, ranked by priority,' she said.

"'Whose priority?'

"'Mine for now. Of course, I'll review with Jane and let her decide. We'll have to reduce scope, pretty severely.'

"'I can see that,' I said.

"'Because there are so many interfaces we have to be careful, of course.'

"'Recommendations?' I said.

"'Ask for more time, and money. There's no other way.'

"Her automatic response, what Chuck or Joyce or others would have come up with. I'm sure by now even Missy understood that wasn't feasible, so I let it pass. And she didn't press it either. We assembled a plan, which we were to present to the entire project team in a special meeting.

"I opened by declaring this was the most challenging project I had ever worked on. I reminded them we were in it together and then spouted some other sugar-coating crap. I almost choked on my speech when I saw all the blank faces. No lame pep talk would inspire these indifferent souls. They had experienced all this before, though perhaps not to this degree. I stopped and dove straight into our modified plan, directing them to stop immediately on the cut items to focus on the priority ones. For many it was good news in that it reduced their workload to a more achievable amount.

"That was the easy part. Next, I had to present this plan to the Steering Committee whose reaction would be unpredictable save that it would be negative. I was surprised when Clay showed up. But more so when the development managers, conspicuously low-key since my return, did so too, causing Stu Cairns to ask:

"'Isn't Dustin your prime representative?'

"'Yes, he is,' Fortnum said.

"'Well then, why do we need all these people here?'

"For some reason Fortnum looked at me. Did he think I wanted them at this meeting, or any meeting for that matter? Stu was right, but that was not my battle, so I kept quiet and let Fortnum deal with his counterpart.

"'We're at a critical juncture,' Clay said, 'and I just want to make sure we have the right people here, the ones who can respond directly to any questions you may have.'

"'I've been satisfied with Dustin to this point. Has something changed?'

"Fortnum looked uncomfortable and it was clear he hadn't anticipated this kind of resistance from Cairns. He looked at me again.

"'Dustin, I think you wanted them here too, didn't you?'

"At another time I would have been annoyed at Fortnum for putting me in this position and would have responded glibly. This time I was amused, with no desire to be petty.

"'Doesn't matter to me whether they're here or not.'

"'Never mind then, let's get on with it,' Stu said, 'let's hear what Dustin has to say.'

"And so I broke the news, which was not well received. Neither were my recommendations, which were mostly about reducing the project's scope. The moment I stopped talking a blame fest broke out. Accusations were hurled left and right but I stayed out of it. With no authority, I bore no accountability. I couldn't resist an occasional smirk at the terrible look on the faces of Chuck and Joyce once they realized they were there only to act as Fortnum's shields. After about ten minutes of this, Stu Cairns's voice came through and his words shut everyone up.

"'My instinct tells me I should cut our losses and cancel this fiasco.'

"This alternative, always looming but never openly stated till then, quieted the room. For me the idea offered hope of relief, as a prisoner might feel just before a parole hearing, even though he has no life to go to on the outside. An ominous silence followed as Stu looked at me.

"'But I won't, not yet. We'll go with Dustin's revised plan but it had better damn well work.'

"'I understand,' I said.

"'I hope so. The way I see it you now have the same amount of time to test as before, but you're only testing a small bit. If anything, you should finish early.'

"From his perspective, that made sense. Since his perspective was the only one that mattered, I chose not to point out that because our new scope required taking out already tested components, the testing complexity had actually increased.

"Keeping quiet was a good call. After that I enjoyed a stretch of peace as development went on, relatively uninterrupted, and we actually completed our first phase.

"IT had first crack at verifying that all the pieces in the system integrated seamlessly and functioned as expected. We assembled a team of testers from a pool of developers who had not worked on the project to ensure test integrity. A process—created by Jacques—was implemented for consistency in defect identification and resolution.

"Not surprisingly, his methods optimized bureaucracy over simplicity. Within a week, a variety of defect reports clogged the process. It was impossible to track who was fixing what, who was testing what, under what version of software, and so on. Two weeks passed before testing regained momentum. We managed to meet the dates of the signoff schedule upright, but limping, with temporary workarounds to deal with several major mechanical defects and a few dozen minor ones. A long and heated quality control discussion took place with Jane's team and it was agreed business testing would begin as planned the following day, with the existing known defects.

"Only two days into her team's testing, Jane called an emergency meeting. Seeing the other attendees were the usual suspects—Chuck, Joyce, and Missy—gave me no indication of the context. Everyone else seemed to know though and that annoyed me so I sat in a corner, brooding.

"'It doesn't work,' Jane said.

"'Have you reported it as a defect?' Joyce said.

"'Defect? The whole thing doesn't work. We can enter orders but they go nowhere.'

"Ted Scholes entered the room then. He said hello to Chuck and Joyce, sat between them, and was then introduced to Jane. He avoided me and I wondered why he'd be there. My stomach churned and I longed for that giant bottle of antacids I often saw on Chuck's desk.

"'Ted, Jane was just saying that the order transport interface doesn't work,' Chuck said.

"Now I perked up. The order transport was the primary interface for the entire application and this was the first I'd heard of troubles with it. When I said as much, everyone became quiet. Missy and Chuck shifted in their seats while Jane sat in the back in bored indignation. Joyce was looking smug while Ted had his face turned down.

"'I'm sure it's just some configuration problem,' Ted said.

"'That's what I've been saying,' Joyce said, who then turned to Jane and smiled.

"'Don't worry, just leave it to us, it'll be up and going shortly,' Ted said.

"'When?' Jane said, her voice suspicious.

"Joyce looked at Ted who looked at Missy who looked at Chuck. I really must have been invisible.

"'We'll, put our best people on it, right away,' Chuck said.

"'No matter the cost,' Ted said.

"'Will someone tell me what's going on?' I said, and then pointed at Ted. 'Will someone tell me why he's here? He has nothing to with the inter—oh no.' Everyone turned to me. 'Goddamn it, you bastard, you purchased that crappy middleware product after all.'

"'It's not a crappy product,' Ted said.

"He then explained that during scope cutting, a vendor demonstrated how their product could function as the interface, how it was a faster solution, and how it was a solution more in line with the grand schemes of Ted and his buddies. Apparently, as soon as the salesman's words matched the brochure verbiage, Ted was sold. He and the other architects proceeded to implement it on a free trial so it flew under my budgetary radar. |When the software problem surfaced, and was found to be a fault with the product, nothing could be done. We had no warranty and a fix would have to wait until we purchased it.

"'Missy, what will it take to pull it out and replace it with what we developed?' I said.

"Her eyes lit up and it looked like she was on my side, but before she could speak Chuck raised his hand.

"'We can't pull it out,' he said.

"'Why not?' I said.

"'Because, all our code has been written specifically for this product,' Joyce said. 'We had no choice, given the time constraints.'

"'Is this what you mean by a flexible architecture?' I said, my eyes fixed on Ted.

"I left the room then, not waiting for an answer, before I would explode. Later that day, after a long lunch and a few beers, I presented these circumstances to Stu."

1101

"And I promptly shut down Project Melange," Stu Cairns says.

Dustin takes a long drink of wine, the guttural swish seeming to echo in the quiet room as he observes the others. Their faces remain impassive, impossible to read. Was he really expecting more? A closer, second look reveals, on Fisher's face, a mild, cold expression, bordering on smugness. Bradfield and Megan maintain a calm, stoic, professional demeanour; they don't seem one bit dissatisfied with either his tale or the reaction.

After a minute of silence, Bradfield clears his throat, looks at each of the attendees before addressing Wenham.

"Now do you still consider our approach drastic?"

Slowly, Wenham shakes his head, as the waiters return with trays of desserts.

In her office the next day, Megan reveals the details of her intricate plan to Dustin. It calls for Dustin to return to DexiaTel to work in Stu Cairns's Customer Operations department under Deepak, who is heading a group under Jane Gooden that's currently paralleling IT activities. Dustin will act behind the scenes, as a consultant, using a false identity, in a satellite office. Cassandra will be there to help him. Jane will be kept unaware of who Dustin is at first, as will Marty Tellerini who will have returned from a leave of absence not unlike Dustin's own exile. Marty will cross over from IT to join Deepak's group. Once comfortable with Marty, Dustin will divulge to the younger man the details, including his identity and role.

The real action will begin with Wenham's announcement of Fortnum's dismissal, with no replacement named. In the subsequent chaos, Marty will act as Dustin's eyes and ears while Deepak's people agitate Fortnum's managers, goading them, confusing them into a state of disarray, which will keep them occupied while all the administrative work to retrofit the IT organization is completed.

The plan is not limited to IT. All the members of Jane's team, except for those working with Deepak, will be sent away on a course. During their absence, there will be a giant assembly where Dustin will reveal himself to the IT department and make the announcements. When Jane's team returns from their course, they will clean up the residue from those IT employees, before they too will be let go. Finally, Dustin will reveal everything to Jane and help her build the new IT department until she can take it over fully.

The ambitious plan, as he'd expect from Megan, is detailed and comprehensive—employees are named with no one unaccounted for—and adaptable to unforeseen circumstances, such as Dustin's participation.

Yet something nags at him. All this work, all this complexity, just to sweep away the deadwood while trying to cause the least impact to existing work. A bureaucratic magic trick, like snapping away the tablecloth without removing the plates, glasses, and cutlery first.

"What do you think?" Megan says.

"I love the drama, the intricacy, the secrecy."

"Thank you," she says, "but . . ."

"But, it's not drastic enough. It's too slow."

"What do you suggest?"

"Fire all the managers and put me in charge," he says.

"All of them, all at once? As simple as that?"

"Megan, you don't fight bureaucracy with intricacy; you fight it with simplicity."

He sees the doubt in her eyes. As brilliant as Megan is, she has not lived his experience. She cannot see what he's seen, cannot fathom the depths Fortnum and all those with him have brought his people to. Dustin can because he sees it another way, sees it by looking at the work they do. Removing Chuck, Joyce, and all the rest will do no harm because the work they do has no value. Since the merger, there has not been one project, one venture, one initiative that has significantly benefited the company. All the work for what? To look big? To support a bureaucracy?

As he tries to explain, as much to himself as to Megan, Bradfield enters. The owner of Paleo Transitions doesn't take the time to remove his coat, nor to brush off the snow.

"We've lost a client," he says, his tone matter-of-fact. "There's been a takeover at DexiaTel."

"I had a feeling," Megan says.

"Wenham's out and Miranda Fisher is temporary CEO, though I suspect it'll become permanent. All other personnel changes have been frozen indefinitely. Fortnum remains where he is. No idea what's happened to Stu."

"Remarkable," Megan says.

"Yes. It's my understanding the new owners intend to convert DexiaTel into an income trust. The focus will be on low-risk profitability, the established customer base. So much for innovation."

"Just as well," Dustin says, "that's really all it's been for a long time."

"What do you mean?" Bradfield says.

"Like I was telling Megan just now. All those failed projects, all those idealistic architectures, all those meetings; DexiaTel's been nothing more than a make-work environment, a middle-class welfare system."

"I'm sorry, Dustin," Megan says. "I imagine you were looking forward to setting many things right."

"Don't worry about me," Dustin says. "I can no longer begrudge any one of them for taking advantage of that." He looks up at Bradfield. "I'll bet you'll take a big revenue hit over this."

Bradfield puts a hand on his shoulders and flashes the most conniving smile Dustin's ever seen. "My friend, that's why we put in hefty penalty clauses in all our contracts. I always doubted they'd go through with it. I was surprised we'd gotten this far."

Dustin puts on his overcoat, mumbles something about needing some fresh air. No one stops him as he goes down the elevator and out the door into a flurry-whitened world.

FOOD

The businessman pats his bulging stomach, declares his desire to see a menu right away to the hostess, a competent-looking blonde. She gives him a courteous smile, followed by a sombre shake of her pretty head.

"I just handle the bar for Bytes. A food server will be by presently. Until then, something to drink?"

He requests a large draught beer, a light beer, and watches her depart. She returns moments later with a large, icy mug that she places in front of him on a cork coaster she pulls from her back pocket.

"I'll run a tab," she says.

He protests, intending to have only one.

"We'll see," she says.

A trace of irony in her chuckle echoes uneasily in his mind as he enjoys the beer. He glances around at the diner's conventional, unimaginative interior. Walls painted a variety of pastel yellows, mauves, blues, from which hang forgettable pictures of trees, flowers, and plants. As if the owner had shopped from an upscale industry catalogue but purchased only the least expensive items.

His glass is half-empty when a nervous youth arrives. He's wearing an ill-fitting blazer covering a slightly wrinkled shirt. The lad also has a habit of keeping his eyes down while speaking but raising them obsequiously between sentences. He introduces himself not as a waiter, but as a Dining Analyst, or DA, for short.

The businessman restates his wish for a menu. The waiter, or whatever he's calling himself, lowers his hands to his belt before folding them together, fingers twitching slightly.

"You haven't dined at Bytes before, have you, sir?"

The businessman shakes his head, drinks some beer.

"You see, we have no menu," the youth says, and then pauses, as if in awe of this revelation. The unimpressed businessman remains stoically silent and now the DA unclasps and clasps his hands several times.

"What I'm saying is, we have implemented a brand new ordering and serving system. The benefit to our customers of this innovative, advanced approach is that we can serve anything. Any food. In any combination. Furthermore, we can tailor your meal specifically to what you want to spend. It's the ultimate in dining flexibility, a revolutionary breakthrough in the restaurant world, a new paradigm. We at Bytes humbly call it, The Logical Choice. TLC."

The businessman is too hungry to bother with such distinctions. He's been making decisions all day. The beer is making him light-headed, and he barely registers the words as the server prattles on.

"How it works is you tell us exactly what you want to eat. We assess your selection and come back with estimates for price and preparation time. If our assessment meets your approval, you sign, pay, and we proceed to prepare the meal. If, for whatever reason, you change your mind about something—whether a food item, size, quantity, cooking preferences—you inform us and we modify the assessment. If the change is a big one, we'll create a new assessment. It's a collaboration that ensures the meal you get is a perfect balance of cost, convenience, and culinary satisfaction."

The Dining Analyst produces a colourful booklet, which he places in front of the businessman. The laminate cover displays a collage of potatoes, fruits, eggs, breads, meats and, superimposed over these images, in ornate lettering, running diagonally from top left to bottom right: FOOD.

A table of contents lists numerous sections: Introduction, Background, Context, Responsibilities, Revision History, and so on. The Introduction declares this as version 4.7.3.9.1 and reveals FOOD is an acronym: Flexible Omnifarious

Ordering Document. Omnifarious? The Background explains the Latin origin of the word: a combination of all and doing. But nothing in the document even remotely resembles a menu.

The bar girl's chuckle and remark echoes in the businessman's mind. He asks about today's specials.

"Again, you are thinking of a conventional eating establishment. Don't feel bad, it's a common error. But we have no daily specials, per se. To us, every meal is a special. I know the document doesn't spell this out in precisely that way—I believe the next edition will correct that—but I'm sure you'll agree with me that the implication is obvious."

Not to hungry people in a hurry it isn't, but the businessman quells that thought and instead tells the young man he wants a steak, medium-rare, preferably between twelve and sixteen ounces, with potatoes and vegetable. It doesn't matter what kind of vegetable or potato. Hell, any steak will do, for that matter. He just wants it to taste good and to come quick.

"Sir, I must apologize if my explanation wasn't adequate. I can't, of course, take your order verbally. I need to have you write it down. This way we have a physical record that ensures no misinterpretation. This is clearly spelled out. We're about accountability as much as we are about flexibility."

The Dining Analyst extracts a sheet from a folder stapled to the inside back cover of the FOOD. He produces a pen and places both items delicately between the businessman and his beer. Except for the bold-faced letterhead and the title below it—Customer Order Form—the sheet is blank. The businessman stares at it for several seconds, clicks the pen several times, and then starts to write.

"And please be as specific as possible. Precision is important. On page thirty-six of the FOOD there is a special section to help with tricky spellings."

The businessman stops, gazes straight ahead, thinks about saying something. Instead, he waits until the DA leaves. He writes what he told the young man a moment earlier, verbatim, in large letters, making one change to qualify the vegetable as green. Satisfied, the businessman pushes the sheet to the edge of the table, finishes his beer, signals to the cute girl for another, which he gets promptly.

The completed form sits unacknowledged for several minutes and the businessman wonders if it is up to him to bring it somewhere. The way things are going he wouldn't be surprised. He picks it up and then, for no reason, flips it over. On the reverse, it looks like a multiple-choice test: boxes to check breakfast, lunch or dinner, another three to select an entree price range: $10-20, $20-50, $50-200, $200 and higher! A greyed out area is reserved for someone called a Culinary Architect, with a warning in capital letters not to write anything there. Two lines for the date and a signature, cushioned by several paragraphs of ominous small print, fill the bottom of the document. The businessman completes the second page but chooses not to sign; he never signs anything before knowing the cost.

When he explains this to the Dining Analyst, the young man seems perplexed, but only for a moment.

"Ah, I see. No, it's okay to sign. This is not a commitment to the order, only the first step in compiling it. Your signature at this point will not involve any cost. Yes, I know it may appear pointless but, well, signatures are necessary at each stage. The cost will be clear and finalized once the kitchen completed the meal assessment."

Partially mollified, but completely hungry, the businessman signs. The DA takes the paper and skims the first page, frowns but then leaves when he gets no reaction.

Another beer goes down and the businessman catches the bar girl's eye. She winks good-naturedly, points at the beer tap. He nods. In a few seconds, with fresh frosted glass in hand, he sits back and sighs. At least the beer is cold.

And the cold beer puts him in a more tolerant frame of mind. While what they're doing at Bytes is bizarre, he concedes that trying to offer everything is ambitious. He admires ambition. Perhaps, under different circumstances, he would be more imaginative and order something extravagant.

The Culinary Architect smacks the paper with the back of his hand, scowls at the tear, and then at the Dining Analyst.

"This is no good. You'll have to take it back."

"Why, what's wrong?"

This results in a heavy sigh.

"What's wrong? What isn't wrong? I don't even know where to begin. What kind of steak does he want? And here, where it says green vegetable. Well, we have them all—peas, beans, string beans, celery, broccoli, seven kinds of endive, Brussels sprouts—there are so many green vegetables. Which one? We don't have the time to choose or guess. And there's nothing about dessert. You know better than this."

The DA nods and contains his irritation with this Culinary Architect who, of them all, is the strictest. Easy for him, the DA thinks, insulated inside the kitchen. He ought to try it out there in the dining room once. See how he handles all those bewildered customers.

"And look at this," the CA says. "He's marked the box for lunch, when it should be supper. It's already past four o'clock, for crying out loud."

"It's just a mistake, that's all. We can change it."

The Culinary Architect hands back the form. "It's a mess."

"It's okay. It's not ripped too badly. I can tape it up."

"What? No. I mean how it's filled out, or rather not filled out."

"Okay, okay, I get it. Look, can't you cut me some slack? This guy looks so hungry I think he'll eat anything we give him, as long as it comes out quickly and tastes reasonably good."

"I don't care. We can't cook a single thing until we know what it is we're going to cook. With what you gave me, there's no way I can even price the meal, let alone start cooking it."

"How about a ballpark figure of the cost and how long it might take, something I can bring back?"

"No."

"Then what should I say to the customer?"

"Hey, that's your problem. I just prepare the meals. It's your responsibility to get all the information in the first place."

"Yeah, yeah, yeah."

"Hey, did you ever think that this guy might be a mole, from head office, here to test how we are doing under the new processes? You wouldn't want to cut any corners then, would you? Would you? Would you? No, I didn't think so."

"Sir, I'm afraid I have to ask you to write out your order again."

The businessman slams his glass down. A puddle of foam and beer forms on the table and he glares at the Dining Analyst as if the spill is the server's fault. With a trembling hand, the DA wipes the table and reaches for a new order form and pen, miraculously without dropping either.

"I—we—know that you want a steak, potato, and vegetable. We just need to be more precise about the details. After all, we want your meal to be perfect, exactly meeting your requirements."

The businessman sighs, rolls his eyes, takes the pen and paper, and then motions for the DA to remain until he finishes.

"Steak . . . any kind you like . . . Porterhouse . . . yes, of course we can do that. And how you want . . . medium-rare . . . perfect . . . just put that down, yes right there . . . potato . . . whichever you like sir . . . no, I can't give a recommendation, it should be—baked potato—good, an easy one—no, it's es, not s, I think . . . yes, just write . . . the vegetable? Again, we have them all—something green? . . . a list? I'm afraid I can't really do that . . . if you have a fav— broccoli—perfect . . . suggest you also choose a dessert too . . . you're not sure yet . . . but we do need to get something down now . . . strawberry cheesecake, terrific, I've had it mys—yes, of course you might change your mind. That's your prerogative. We'll cross that bridge when we come . . . great and, oh, you need to sign, wonderful . . . thank you."

"Appetizers," the Culinary Architect says, releasing one of derogatory sighs. "There's nothing here about appetizers. I don't want to hear afterwards that we never offered appetizers."

"Isn't it implied? I mean, if he didn't write it down, he doesn't want any, wouldn't you think?"

The Dining Analyst holds his breath. He's tried this argument before, with mixed success, and never with this Culinary Architect. After contemplating several seconds, and scraping two large knives together, the CA shakes his head.

"No. We must have it written down. If it's written down, we're protected."

"Protected?"

"Yes, protected. Do you know how often it's happened that a customer says one thing and then claims they said something different after the fact?"

"I've never seen it happen here."

"No, not here, dummy. It can't happen here. That's one of the benefits of TLC for us. It gives us protection as long as we don't stray. And if we're protected it means all customers are served equally. At the end of the day it's about pleasing the customer."

"I don't think this customer will change his mind."

"Oh? Oh? You don't think—listen—I've been around a lot longer than you have. That's one of the reasons we were compelled to design a comprehensive process like this. Without it, you'd appreciate why we can't make any exceptions; because of it, you may never have to."

A feeling of futility and dejection almost overcomes the DA. The Culinary Architect puts down his knives to huddle with him, speaking in a conspiratorial whisper.

"Tell you what. He doesn't have to do all of it over. Just get him to write 'No appetizer', if that's his wish, and then get him to initial it. Hell, I'll sign off even if you write the words yourself, as long as they're his initials. But they must be his initials, got it? I'll know if they're not."

The businessman steps away for a change of atmosphere. The same girl is still behind the bar. She really is quite striking, better looking each round. A fresh draft, accompanied by her charming company, cheers him up. His eyes drift to several columns of potato chips clipped to a rotating metal holder. He crinkles one of the packages and then checks the due date stamped on the wrapper. To his surprise, each is fresh.

"They're quite popular," the girl says. "We go through at least two cases a day."

He asks if she ever eats in the diner. She points to a brown paper bag in the corner by the coffee / espresso machine. Jokingly, he offers her fifty dollars for it.

"Not a chance," she says, unsmiling.

He returns to his table when he sees the Dining Analyst moping like a lost child in a shopping mall. A piece of paper dangles between the young man's twitchy fingers. The businessman deliberately avoids eye contact as he sits down.

"Just another thing, sir. Can I assume you do not want an appetizer?"

The businessman nods and the DA hastily scribbles something.

"Then could I just ask you to initial this?"

The businessman glares at the youth. The DA flinches, but only briefly. Their eyes lock for several seconds before the businessman grabs the paper and pen, locates the scribbled words, signs his initials. He mumbles something about trust and customers but the DA's mind seems elsewhere.

The Dining Analyst returns to the kitchen to find the Culinary Architect busy with a new staff member, explaining, cajoling, and eventually consoling. He waits patiently and reflects on the stare-down with the customer.

Why couldn't the guy be more understanding, more patient? In what other restaurant can one find such a variety of offerings? Where else can one go and order a hamburger one time, escargot another, and then Chinese food, Italian, or Turkish, not to mention sushi and caviar? Nowhere. Naturally, with flexibility comes minor inconveniences. That was only logical. The Culinary Architect's rigidity is frustrating but, technically, he is correct and only following a process. Just as he, the DA, is trying to do.

The CA grabs the sheet. "Could be better but I'll take it."

The DA breathes a sigh of relief, happy with acceptable, wondering what it would take to exceed this Culinary Architect's standards.

"Any chance you can put a rush on this?" the DA says, but with far less conviction than his previous entreaties.

"I'll see what I can do."

The DA's calm lasts only until he sees the document the CA prepared. He imagines the customer's reaction, but without fear. Instead, he feels a sense of superiority, an odd mix of indifference and something else.

FOOD

Weakened by the beer and an empty stomach, the businessman is almost pleading as he asks where his food might be. The Dining Analyst does not answer but instead places yet another document on the table and points his finger down at the sheet.

"Pending approval, we are ready to prepare the meal. But first, as I stated earlier, we must ensure clarity on all aspects of the order, including price. This is our assessment of your order, and our declaration of commitment."

Another document, another acronym. COOKS this time: Customer Order O K Signoff. Four sheets of paper itemizing the order, ingredient by ingredient, giving approximated cost (+/- 10%), estimated preparation time (+/- 5 minutes), and other information, winding up with a summary on the last page. Below the summary four lines, three already signed.

"As you can see it's been approved by the Culinary Architect, the Chief Culinary Architect, and your Dining Analyst, me. We just need your signature to proceed. You'll be pleased to hear—although you may already know because it's in the FOOD—that this is the last step."

The businessman demands to know whether they've even started cooking his meal yet. The DA shrugs.

"They're not supposed to initiate an order without a completed COOKS document."

He knows it's futile but the businessman once again appeals for a quick meal. The DA remains impassive. When the businessman suggests this whole experience or system or whatever was some kind of bad joke and how none of it made sense the DA shakes his head.

"Of course it makes sense. As you can clearly see, these are your—," but then the businessman stabs his index finger at an item on page three. "Oh yes, the CA feels you don't want broccoli and that carrots would be—"

The businessman curses, tells the Dining Analyst how he hates carrots, did not ask for carrots, did not want carrots, would not eat carrots, and demands the DA, the CA, the Chief CA, the owner, or whoever, change it back.

Instead of arguing, or even acknowledging the outburst, the Dining Analyst leaves, taking the papers with him. Now the businessman regrets his reaction. The vegetable isn't important and he doesn't really hate carrots that much. No matter, as the DA returns in less than a minute. Apparently, the chef, or CA, rejected the broccoli again.

The businessman, face still red, calmly asks to see someone in charge. The DA, in an equally calm voice, explains that the Culinary Architect cannot leave his post, adding that customers are prohibited from entering the kitchen. Any dining room issue must be resolved with the Dining Analyst.

Hunger overpowers the businessman and he tells the DA to forget the carrots. Now he scans the rest of the assessment, longing to sign. He gets as far as the price. He stares at it, performs a mental tally of the individual components, and stares again. Despite his hunger, he cannot refrain protesting the number quoted. His full indignation comes to bear in a histrionic rant about the service, the concept, the delay, his hunger, and to top it all, an outrageous price.

The DA remains unfazed, his face sporting a look that says, "Hey, the longer you take . . ." When the businessman finishes, the DA rhymes off a list of factors contributing to the cost. The businessman listens to them all, believes none, surrenders his credit card, but then pulls it back. He tells the Dining Analyst he's changed his mind about an appetizer, that he wants an order of garlic bread.

"Of course. You know we want your meal to come out exactly as you wish. Just fill out another order sheet and I'll take care of the rest."

It annoys the businessman that the form proves easy to fill out this time. He even remembers to sign. The Dining Analyst takes the form, and the credit card, and returns shortly with a revised estimate. The businessman signs this without a word.

Alone again, the idea of food still seems an impossible dream, even though he's paid for it. There is still his beer, so sympathetic, so understanding, his only friend. He finishes another and then another—sadly, the beautiful girl at the bar has left—until his famished inebriation reaches such an extreme he fears becoming faint. He flags down the DA and requests a meal status.

"I realize you're hungry, please be patient. It's a complex meal, with the requested changes. Fear not though, we will deliver your meal within the committed time range."

Committed time? There was something about time in one of the documents but the businessman cannot remember. He rifles through the stack but cannot find it.

Would it make any difference now?

The businessman stands up and feels dizzy. He leans on the table to regain his balance, takes a long look toward the kitchen. Seeing no sign of the waiter, he goes to the bathroom. When he returns he can't believe his eyes: a plate with food that's food, not an acronym for some ridiculous document. The Dining Analyst is nowhere to be seen.

Disappointment returns when he sees he's been served chicken teriyaki with mashed potatoes and zucchini—no garlic bread—in a bland presentation. It doesn't taste bad although now he senses an unidentifiable aftertaste, a bitter tang that not even the last of the pale ale can neutralize. But at least his hunger is satisfied and he can get back to a rational world.

But he ought to do one last thing and so he sits back down. A thorough inspection of the FOOD reveals that, amongst all the forms and other superfluous information, there is no customer comment card.

GREENER GRASS

Happy Hour at The Ambassador was counting down for Todd Richfield. His waitress chewed her gum as she twirled her gold necklaces with the fingers of one hand. Her other hand balanced a tray of empty beer glasses and bottles.

"So c'mon, what's it gonna be?" she said, nodding toward another table clamouring for her attention.

Todd couldn't decide whether to order a pint for his friend or not, whether to risk Stewart grousing over paying full price or over a warm beer. Each month now it seemed Stewart was trying to set a new lateness record. Maybe it only seemed that way this time because Todd was anxious to share his news. If they didn't have such particular and contrary tastes in beer, he could simply order a pitcher, or two of something. But Todd couldn't stand Guinness, and Stewart felt the same about Todd's Coors Light.

"Well?" the waitress said, in a way that threatened her tip in Todd's mind.

"Just a pint of Coors Light, please," Todd said.

"You won't be needing this chair then?"

"Yes, I will," Todd said. "My friend should be arriving shortly."

He, along with several other men, watched the waitress walk away. It wasn't her personality that would earn her tip.

"Is this seat taken?"

Todd turned around. A smiling man in his thirties, surrounded by three young, possibly underage, girls had two hands clutched on the back of the empty chair.

"Sorry," Todd said, but didn't feel bad when they walked away grumbling. Stewart would show up eventually; he always did.

For nearly seven years now, the two have come to The Ambassador to enjoy cheap drinks and to share respective office war stories. They were part of a large group at one time, at least a dozen people. But with marriages and children and downsizing and new opportunities, the gathering had dwindled both in participation and frequency. The weekly event became biweekly and finally monthly by the time only Todd and Stewart remained. Both men continued the tradition more out of habit than from a general kinship. Todd always held the hope, and he figured Stewart did too, that some of their old friends would make cameo appearances from time to time.

A heavy distressful wheeze shook Todd from his thoughts. He looked up. Stewart had just plopped his ample butt on the empty stool. Ignoring Todd's hello, Stewart wrestled off his ugly green parka, loosened his tie, got the waitress's attention, and somehow negotiated a last second Happy Hour purchase. Then Stewart removed his fogged-up glasses, thumbed his eyes, and let the bottom of his fists slam the table in rehearsed exasperation.

"Rough week?" Todd said.

"If only they'd prepped us at school for the bozos you have to work with in real life."

"What is it now?" Todd said, shrugging.

But he only half-listened as Stewart backed up his comment with anecdotes, some new ones from the past month, others tired old favourites. Over the years, Todd had learned how to tune out Stewart's little tirades without letting on. The occasional nod and, "uh, huh," did the trick. This time, though, he couldn't manage even that.

"Todd, are you still here? Are you even listening?"

"As always, Stewart, as always."

"You seem to be in another zone, just like you have for the past several months."

Perhaps out of superstition, perhaps lacking confidence, Todd had consciously kept quiet for more than a year about his big project, but now his pride forced it out.

He described to Stewart, in detail, his company's ambitious undertaking to retrofit their billing systems to support other currencies. A Canadian company, all of EMJ's systems had been developed for Canadian customers who paid in Canadian dollars. Expansions and mergers had grown the company and now Marketing had international aspirations. EMJ wisely decided to invest in a lasting solution. The project affected almost every aspect of many departments with clashing interests, such as Sales, Marketing, Revenue, and Accounting and, of course, the IT department. Todd was the only IT Project Manager skilled and experienced enough to tackle it. Still, he needed some luck, which came in the form of a decisive client representative form Accounting, Ann Palowitz.

A watershed moment came when he transferred out a particularly destructive analyst who kept trying to steer the project toward irrelevancies, such as increasing the precision of decimal places for interest rate calculations. Another critical but surprisingly controversial decision was to exclude volatile currencies such as those from Turkey, Venezuela, and others. Including them would have entailed a formidable cost increase for development and testing. By sticking together, he and Ann won these battles and the project finished only a month later than the original target date.

"I've never seen you talk about work in such a way," Stewart said.

"What way?"

"I don't know. With such joy."

"I tell you, Stewart, this project was arguably the high point of my career."

"I can't even remember the last project we finished."

"Oh, come on. You must be joking."

"Fourteen months, huh? You must have cut corners. Everyone likes to cut corners. You cut corners, didn't you?"

Todd smiled. "Not at all, we made sure there were no corners to cut."

"What the hell does that mean?"

"It means we focused on necessary things, important things, not features."

"That's just a fancy way of saying you cut corners."

"Oh brother, but hey, that's not all. I have other news—"

A tinny version of Beethoven's ninth symphony began playing.

"Hold on," Stewart said. "Get me another when she comes by, will you?

While Stewart fished around his coat pocket for his cell phone, Todd considered his friend's pessimistic reaction: how bad was the environment at Verdant to warrant such chronic cynicism? In a way, Todd felt a strange envy of Stewart and his chaotic miseries. Sure, he'd succeeded with the last project, but it was somewhat boring, too easy in the end. Maybe that was the true reason he had decided to leave EMJ Telecom, not to depart on a high note as he had told his colleagues, but out of some masochistic need for a different type of challenge.

"So, it looks like we'll be working together," Stewart said, his face beaming.

Todd sipped his beer and grinned. "I know."

"What, how the hell could—who told you?"

"Is that what your call was about?" Todd said.

"Yeah, I was desperately waiting for it. That's why I was kind of miserable when I got here."

"And that call told you we would work together?"

"It did. I start on Monday."

"A transfer?" Todd said.

"No, I'm leaving Verdant for EMJ Telecom. Didn't I just say we're going to work together?"

The waitress came by then and Todd flagged her down.

Scattered documents and computer printouts stacked criss-cross, some bound, some loose, covered most of the desk. Orphaned paper clips, ripped rubber bands and unspent staples littered much of the remaining space, joining pens, pencils, erasers, markers—regular and dry erase in a rainbow of colours—note pads coloured yellow, purple, green, white, sticky and regular, titled with the curly 'V' from the company logo. In the center, a fast food store napkin smudged with an unidentifiable colour lidded a neglected coffee mug. The locked cabinets had no keys. Someone had even taken the chair.

An inauspicious welcome, Todd thought; small wonder no one had offered to escort him to his cubicle. Even the three others sharing the space had vacated prior to his arrival, their monitors flickering screensavers of words, cartoons, and dissolving family photos. The vacuumed floor made the desk appear toxic.

"Inherited quite a mess, eh?"

Todd turned around. A man in his early forties, wearing black Dockers and a light green golf shirt and sipping coffee from an oversized Expo '67 stone mug.

"Excuse me?" Todd said.

"Not just figuratively, but literally too," he said, and then put out his hand. "I'm Wayne Kostas."

"Todd Richfield."

"Somebody should have cleaned up for you. But I guess no one wanted to touch it. Just like no one wants to touch his projects."

"Huh? Whose projects?"

"Stewart Callahan's. Your predecessor."

Hearing his friend's name spoken with such contempt triggered a blurry mental collage of Ambassador anecdotes about colleagues, particularly a recurring theme of their tendency to blame everything on Stewart.

Todd refrained from defending his absent friend. He and Stewart, once over the irony of the switch, had agreed to keep hidden their association from everyone, old and new, until the next time they met at the Ambassador. Now Todd was glad they had also agreed to skip a month so that they could compare meaningful notes and not just first impressions. He laughed nervously, and tried to smile.

"You mean to say Stew—this guy, he left it this way?"

"Oh yeah. Like he left everything, although, not like he had much choice, eh?"

"I don't understand."

"Nope, no choice at all," Kostas said, smirking as he walked away.

Todd waited until Kostas was out of sight before he found a chair in a meeting room and sat at his desk. The exchange continued to disturb him. Had Stewart left on his own as he had implied or was there more to his departure? Was this the type of challenge Todd was looking for? Instead of seeking an answer, he began clearing the filth from the desk and tidying the area up.

He found a thick black binder, slightly bending into the right partition in a conspicuously uncluttered section of the desk. It contained an organized summary of each of Stewart's projects—seven in all—solving acronyms, giving two page descriptions, names of sponsors and contacts and resources, status reports, process forms, and other data, such as meeting details. Three were scheduled for that day.

While the black binder ensured he wouldn't miss any meetings, it provided no code or key to the piles of documentation he had inherited. Todd scanned a few title pages and tables of contents, hoping there would be duplicates or obsolete versions. None was. Self-doubt crept in as he went to his first meeting.

That meeting, beyond providing an introduction to the people he would work with, proved pointless. Once his new colleagues' curiosity about Todd was satisfied, they fidgeted a lot and discussed little, each anxious to return to their other duties. Oddly, even though it wasn't his meeting, everyone seemed to need Todd's blessing before leaving. The other two meetings were the same. He went home feeling empty.

The next day, though, Todd awoke with renewed vigour. Making full use of the recycling bins in the hall, he attacked the mountain of paper. This process of skimming and chucking took several days, during which he discovered five of the seven projects could be set aside to concentrate on two big ones. Not only did this eliminate two-thirds of the paperwork, it cleared half the meetings.

No one complained when he cancelled them.

There was one meeting, not documented in the black binder, which Todd only heard about from Kostas in an offhand discussion ten minutes before it was to begin.

The room was too small. Ten people crowded an oval table designed for eight, with twice as many more surrounding them against the walls. Yet the biweekly departmental Project Overview had the air of a formidable event. Kostas had warned Todd that, while scheduled for two hours, the session rarely took less than three as they reviewed and discussed, in depth, every major issue of every ongoing project affecting the team.

At the first one, Todd was bewildered; at the second, things began to make sense, albeit in a nonsensical way; and at the third, after two people had just spent a half hour discussing issue fourteen of sixty-five, from project three of seven, only to once again defer a resolution, Todd coughed once and the room became silent.

"For two weeks I've listened to a lengthy discussion on this issue, the same discussion because nothing's changed.

Nothing's worse, nothing's better. If it's so important, why don't the interested parties use this meeting time to resolve it, independently? And if it's not important, then close the issue."

An impassive silence. Todd was tempted to shrink away and let his challenge die out. Until he saw in some faces what he interpreted as an appeal, a sign that he was not the only one who felt this way.

"Well, what do you say?" Todd said.

"But this meeting is to discuss all issues," Kostas said, his tone more dialectic than confrontational.

"Okay, but, of all the people here, only two are directly affected by this one."

"But maybe we're all interested," Kostas said.

"Really?" Todd said, not sure it wasn't a trap. "I'm not, and my guess is that most of us here feel the same way. Sure, we may be interested in the answer, but this isn't like school where you have to show the teacher how you got the results. I suggest we let Jeff and Linda leave and spare us the details until there's something worth reporting."

The room became quiet again and Todd felt a chill. Perhaps his presumptuousness offended them, coming so soon from a newbie. Perhaps he had gone too far and misread Kostas.

"Todd's right," Kostas said. "This should be a review, not the place to work things out."

The meeting concluded at that point with most people agreeing to suspend it for a few weeks after Todd accepted the task to recommend another approach. Afterward, Todd sought out Wayne and thanked him for his support.

"No, Todd, thank you."

"What for?"

"The hope."

"Hope? Hope for what?"

"The hope of ridding Verdant of the legacy of Stewart Callahan."

Todd arrived later than usual, Stewart earlier. It was St. Patrick's Day and The Ambassador had a special on pitchers of green beer. The two friends, for once, drank the same beer. Despite the festive atmosphere, they imbibed in silence for two-thirds of the pitcher, except for the occasional comment about the coldness of the beer, the weather, and the waitress's short skirt and top with its strategically placed clovers. When the second round arrived, both men relaxed.

"Hope I didn't leave you a mess at EMJ," Todd said, edging forward.

"Well, since you bring it up," Stewart said, "remember that billing project you talked about last month?"

"Of course I do. What about it?"

"You were pretty much gloating, if I recall."

"Gloating? Proud, yes, but I'm sure I wasn't gloating."

"Okay, okay, never mind."

"What about the project then?"

"I uncovered problems."

"What problems?"

"Some issues, missed," Stewart said, with a serpent-like hiss on the last syllable. "Funny how no one ever set up a formal issues log."

"Didn't need one, Stewart."

"Don't be so sure."

"What do you mean? Are you saying the clients aren't happy?"

"No, nothing like that."

"Then what's your point?"

"If you must know, there is one major issue, so far."

"At last," Todd said, and filled his glass from the pitcher, but not filling Stewart's, which was almost empty.

"It's the exchange rate precision."

"Oh?"

"You know, when you deal in large amounts of money, you need to round up accurately."

"I know that," Todd said. "What's the issue?"

"Yeah, of course, well, you know, four digits aren't enough. We need six decimal places, to be safe."

"Oh Stewart, don't fall for that red herring. That idea originated with some imbecilic, meddling director and it took me a long time to shake it. If I'd given it any credence then I'd still be there working on it."

Stewart drank the rest from his glass, filled it up from the pitcher, and waved to the waitress for more.

"In my opinion, you probably should have waited."

"Sure, why not spend time and money for something that'll never be a problem."

"No need to get sarcastic."

"Listen, Stewart, I know for a fact that no one, absolutely no one, in Accounting wanted six digits."

"Perhaps that's what they said then."

"Are you telling me somebody changed their mind?"

"No, not yet, but soon, when we begin the next phase, I'll point it out and argue for it. I truly believe our systems should be ready in case they ever do. It's kind of like Y2K."

"Y2K? How is that at all like Y2K?"

"Sorry if I've offended you, Todd. Why not return the favour and tell me about Verdant. Give it to me straight, I can take it. Trust me, there's nothing you can say that I wouldn't have heard before."

"It's clear you had plenty of influence there."

"Absolutely. But what about the people? How are you coping with them?"

"Fine."

"How about Kostas? Have you had to deal with him yet?"

"Yep."

"Lazy jerk. Always gave me a hard time."

Todd lifted his beer glass in front of his mouth, shrugged.

"Boy Todd, you're not very forthcoming today. Hopefully, I can get more out of you next time."

On Monday, when Stewart began designing his issues log, he documented the exchange rate problem as number one. The only issue. But Stewart knew that, with further analysis, he'd uncover more. Then, when the second phase got underway, he'd have a prepared list of items to include, not only giving the team a grasp of what was needed but also a head start on analysis.

However, once Stewart began his investigations, he found it harder to locate problems than he'd anticipated and couldn't help but admire the job Todd had done. That lasted until the end of the week.

For some reason all of the systems indirectly excluded weak currencies. They did this because they assumed no order could exceed nine hundred ninety-nine million currency units. This was reasonable for the dollar, the euro, the pound, the Swiss franc. But what if a Venezuelan customer came along with a multi-billion bolivar order and insisted on doing business in that currency. Or a Turkish conglomerate with trillions of lire; there were many others. Even the Japanese yen was risky for large contracts.

The assumption that such customers themselves would prefer to deal with a stable currency didn't wash with Stewart. Nor the one that said that clients who wanted to avoid a stable currency might prove to be unreliable clients. The last thing anyone wanted was to give Marketing an excuse to blame an IT system for losing a large customer. This became issue number two.

Dismayingly, Stewart's manager seemed bewildered by the issues log and asked Stewart to hold off until the next phase of the project formally kicked off to make his points. Stewart wanted to heed his manager but the matter became so fixed in his mind that he had to address it, even at the risk of insubordination. And so, two weeks prior to the formal start of Phase B, Stewart called a meeting, inviting everyone who'd worked on Phase A, the phase for which Todd was still revered.

Stewart now stood at the front of the large conference room, facing dozens of blank, intractable faces. No worries; he'd faced such complacency many times in his career. Soon they'd see things his way. Besides, after more than two months into his new job, it was about time he started cultivating a degree of influence at EMJ similar to the type he had earned at Verdant. Even Todd had acknowledged that. He cleared his throat to get their attention.

"I've discovered a situation that needs to be addressed as a high priority," he said.

His audience listened patiently. When Stewart finished, everyone kept quiet, until a middle-aged Indian man and a younger Eastern European woman simultaneously raised their hands. Stewart had met them both but couldn't remember their names. He flashed them a patronizing smile. The Indian man, glancing at his colleague's raised hand, put his down to let the woman speak.

"This is a waste of time," she said. "It's not an issue. It was covered with Marketing a long time ago. Todd Richfield got them to signoff."

"I believe it's an issue, an important one," Stewart said.

"Even if it is, such issues should wait until the next phase begins," the woman said, her tone firm but polite, "and be dealt with by that team."

Stewart shook his head. "But Phase B does not cover as much as Phase A did, and so this issue impacts people not impacted by Phase B. So shouldn't everyone be involved?"

"We'd involve them as needed," the woman said.

"How can you know who those people are if you don't maintain a log of issues that identifies an owner and lists impacted areas?" Stewart said, sighing. "And how can you create such a list without a meeting like this?"

The woman shrugged as it to say she had said all she wanted to say and then glanced around the room for others to add something. Other than a couple of groans, no one did.

The lukewarm response did not deter Stewart. After the meeting, he tenaciously pressed his point, vowing to escalate the matter through management. While his superiors did not approve his wish to retrofit all the Phase A work to address the weak currency issue, they did look favourably on his general ideas.

This encouragement sparked a diligent quest to alter the processes at EMJ Telecom to adopt and conform to his methods. Stewart argued that—contrary to current thinking at EMJ Telecom—by thoroughly analyzing, tracking, and resolving all issues, overall efficiency would increase. This was because not all issues were equal. Some took a day, some a few days or a week, but there were those that needed serious analysis that could take months. In those cases, work could proceed on other projects between outcomes. Even though individual projects might take longer, the productivity of the department as a whole would improve.

During his campaign, protests came frequently and several people threatened to complain to their managers and to his manager too. If they did, none of it reached Stewart. The problem, he saw, was that these people were just lazy and had had it easy for too long. It was one of Stewart's tenets that if one's work didn't exceed the forty-hour workweek, one wasn't doing enough.

Most managers, including his own, now felt more involved, more indispensable than before. They agreed with Stewart that the promise of half a dozen projects in the future was better than the certainty of two now.

Apparently, not everyone had been a Todd Richfield fan.

It was only minutes until Happy Hour. Only a handful of people were in The Ambassador when Stewart, for the first time, arrived before Todd. He was anxious to announce the promotion he had received that day.

"You're Stewart Calligan, right?" the waitress said, once he'd taken off his coat.

"Callahan," Stewart said, and then nodded.

"Your friend, Todd, called and says he can't make it. Something about a party for a project just wrapped up."

"I see," Stewart said, taken aback, and for a moment feeling as if he had been cheated of something.

Project? Todd hadn't been at Verdant long enough to finish any of the projects he'd left behind, let alone to start and complete something new. It had to have been a rush job. Then he pictured Todd, struggling to get away from the office, regretting leaving EMJ. Perhaps it was a joke; no way could a project have completed so soon. Or the waitress had misinterpreted the message. That was it. It could have been anything, someone's birthday or a mid-project morale builder.

"So, do you want a beer, or what?" she said.

Stewart looked at his watch and thought of the work he had put off to get to the bar in time for Happy Hour, and shook his head.

CAREER

In the back offices of the popular woman's magazine, Martha Fitzgerald had to interrupt her envelope stuffing when called into her supervisor's office. Ann Parkerson wasn't there though. Behind the desk instead sat her supervisor's boss, the corporate-climbing Cindy Palestro. The youthful manager was wearing her customary prim turtleneck sweater with white flower holding back her hair behind one ear, which made her look much older than her claim of twenty-six.

Cindy flashed Martha a patronizing smile before handing over an envelope. In appreciation of twenty-three years of loyalty to the magazine—Cindy was reading from a letter, not looking at Martha—there would be a generous severance package along with the free services of a company that specialized in finding work for people in her situation.

"This is because of my letter customizations isn't it?" Martha said.

"No," Cindy said, and then explained, in a terse and tired voice, that all functions of Martha's job had been absorbed into a computer system. "It affects everyone in your group."

"And Ann?"

Cindy shook her head grimly, at which point Martha saw her supervisor's family photo taken in Niagara Falls was no longer on the desk.

The amount of the severance allowed Martha to take the news in stride. It helped that Harold—incompetently charming real estate salesman that he was—had actually made three deals in the past two months. They'd be okay. So Martha's concerns turned outward and she provided much appreciated consolation to her less fortunate former co-workers. She hosted a farewell lunch for her team at her house the next day, ordering in pizzas.

The little party, a staid affair at first, picked up when someone took a call on her cell phone. She shared the news that the much-despised Cindy Palestro now shared their fate too. Martha felt a karmic guilt relishing this but joined in the buoyant spirits nonetheless.

The next day two of Harold's deals fell through. And the day after that, she received her final pay statement—the one that included the settlement—minus the unexpected exponential amount of income tax withheld. Instead of the months-long sabbatical she had envisioned, Martha faced pressure to find another job quickly. As she'd taken the magazine job straight out of high school, she'd never had to do this before. The placement company helped.

Two weeks of submitting resumes and letters finally resulted in an interview at another woman's magazine. Martha was waiting in the reception area, along with two other ladies—both younger—when she thought she saw Cindy Palestro exiting the very door Martha was waiting to enter.

The carnation in the woman's hair confirmed it. Martha hid her face behind a newspaper until Cindy was gone. Martha considered leaving; how could she compete with a young go-getter like Cindy Palestro? Of course, she would get it ahead of a middle-aged hag like Martha. The fact that it would be a comedown for the haughty woman brought no pleasure to Martha.

But then the receptionist called for Martha and the interview went very well, so well that, to Martha's surprise, she was hired on the spot.

Six months later, Martha's new employer implemented the same computer system that had replaced her at the other magazine.

This time, as she was still on hiring probation, she received no severance. And Harold was struggling again. Martha updated her resume and went job hunting, landing several interviews but no jobs; either they didn't like her or she didn't like them.

Martha had plenty of time to catch up on her afternoon soaps. One day, during a commercial break, she caught an interview with someone from the local community college who was describing a special computer programming course, a two-year programme compressed into one. Even better, a government initiative would pay tuition for qualified unemployed people. A sign from heaven, it seemed. Although she would have to pay for transportation, food, and books, it was a worthwhile risk.

Martha qualified for the grant but still had to apply for the popular course. She would be accepted, pending an aptitude test every applicant had to pass. She always excelled at these and it came as no surprise to her that she had scored highest. A new life seemed to be inviting her.

But then seeing all the young students on the grounds on her first day at school—so much energy and ambition—Martha became conscious of her age. At forty-seven, it would be daunting to compete for jobs with these kids, some of whom were younger than her children would be, if she and Harold had conceived any. But none of these kids was in her class; her program was a special one targeted to adults. She wasn't even the oldest student.

Martha excelled in the course, impressing her instructors and classmates with her affinity for the logic and structure and orderliness of computer programming. Martha felt more alive in those months than she had the past ten years of typing, filing, and other manual office work put together. She was at or near the top of the class in all her subjects. Why hadn't she done something like this twenty-five years earlier? The gloom of regret preyed on her until one of the instructors pointed out Martha's unique situation.

"Your life experience is an advantage."

"How so?" she said.

"You know what it's like to have a job that's automated by a computer."

And that's when she began to understand the power of computers, and appreciate why the magazines she had worked for had chosen them over her. It was never personal. The computer was not an inanimate enemy, but a tool with humans behind it, as well as in front of it. She knew both sides as well as anyone could.

As the course neared completion and most of the other students, even those whose grades ranked below hers, were landing jobs, Martha had no success. The quizzical eyes of interviewers told her they could not reconcile her age and frumpiness with her transcripts. Whenever she pointed out the advantage her instructor had told her, their confusion cemented and they politely sent her away. It all seemed a waste of time. Harold, despite his sporadic income, started to nag her about it too and she could offer no response to his snide remarks.

Two days before graduation, Martha ran into Cindy in the school's cafeteria. As is often the case in situations like this, surprise combined with unfamiliar context trumped history and the two women greeted each other like old sorority sisters. Cindy, who was there to scout interns, seemed younger (less stressed) and older (mature) at the same time. In a tailored navy skirt and matching jacket, the woman who had fired Martha exuded pure professionalism. It helped that she'd freed her hair from the constraints of those silly flowers.

When Martha revealed how well she had done in the course, Cindy's congratulatory response was sincere. Not a single trace of condescension or acrimony. Under other circumstances, Martha realized, Cindy could have been a friend. After all, hadn't she ended up a victim of the computer too? So she accepted Cindy's offer for a coffee.

Martha brought up spotting Cindy at that job interview a couple of years before. It took a few moments for Cindy to recall and then to reveal that she had been there by mistake, thinking it was for a different job. They had offered Cindy the position before Martha, but she had declined it.

"Where do you work then?" Martha said.

"You'll never believe it."

Cindy told her how she now worked for the company that had sold the computer system that had evicted Martha and her friends from their jobs. A surge of bitterness came over Martha upon hearing this and it must have shown on her face. For then Cindy admitted how firing all of them had been the most difficult thing she had ever had to do in her career. Martha wanted to believe her and she accepted the words at face value. That felt good. As did brushing the apology aside and saying that things always turned out for the best. Cindy agreed.

They parted company on wonderful terms, although Martha never expected to see Cindy again. But she was wrong. Cindy showed up a few weeks later at Martha's graduation, with a job offer. Martha accepted instantly.

Her first assignment as a professional computer programmer was to maintain the part of the system that had automated her job three years before. Martha's specific responsibility, largely due to her personal experience, became the letter writing function.

Oh, the irony.

Now Martha earned five times as much programming the computer what to type as when she typed it. Best of all, since Cindy managed a different department, there was no latent awkwardness. The two women became friends, lunching together at least twice a month.

Cindy proved a great comfort to Martha when Harold decided to leave her for another woman. Martha did likewise by listening sympathetically to Cindy's man troubles, including one particularly delicate office romance. They never talked about the past, especially not about the letter customization Martha still felt was the true reason she lost her job at the first magazine.

Back then, it was normal for Martha to talk to subscribers on the phone and from those calls, she made notes of little details such as birthdays, children and pet names, allergies and sicknesses, hobbies and general concerns women could share. Why not use that information, she thought at the time, to spice up the letters, personalize them? And so she did.

"Dear Mrs. Smith, I hope your tulips are performing well this season. We will soon publish a special gardening series, including a long feature on tulips and how to make them last. Now might be a good time to extend . . ."

Subscribers loved it. Her supervisor loved it. A number of times Ann passed on letters of appreciation from subscribers, many declaring it was Martha's words that had made them renew. Encouraged, Martha often worked late, without overtime, just to get a certain sentiment right. So it came as a shock when Ann—probably passing on Cindy's orders—began to discourage Martha from doing this. She told Martha the magazine was afraid of setting an expectation they might not always be able to meet. To Martha, it seemed counter-intuitive to do anything to distance a subscriber

She continued to think that way until she went to school. Then she saw how the ruthless, impersonal efficiency of the computer demanded simplicity. The complicated logic required to automate her letter customization practices would be formidable.

But was that the case still? Because by now Martha's programming skills had multiplied with experience; formidable had become possible.

On her own time, on nights and weekends, Martha designed a special database to store all kinds of information: data about the particular magazines, keywords and other links to future storylines and announcements; about its customers and their personal circumstances and habits. Some of the data could, using the proper logic, be inferred from other data about the general world: geographical, historical, current affairs, weather, politics, sports, and so on. Then just add on a variety of sentimental adjectives and link them to the type of reader and noun to which they were best suited. Her design was complex but it ensured the function could grow and adapt to the variety of magazines offered by its clients, tailored to their diverse computer systems.

Next Martha had to work out the necessary logic to link her database to the letter writing function. She programmed and tested for a long time. It was tiring but a labour of love. In six months, she could finally make her company's software create letters almost as good as the ones she used to write.

"Dear Ms. Jones, soon you and your Crescent City neighbours will be busy with Mardi Gras, and we just happen to have a special feature on that event in our July issue, so this would be a good time to renew . . . Dear Mrs. Roopsingh, the upcoming eclipse, for which we have a delightful little article, can be seen clearly in your town . . ."

Without informing anyone, Martha installed her change, but only for one client. Naturally, she chose the woman's magazine Martha and Cindy used to work at. Not much had changed in how they operated so it was easy for Martha—now an expert in computers—to figure out the various databases there, which also proved useful in her testing.

Every day for the next two weeks, Martha closely monitored the computer-generated letters to make sure her modifications came out as expected. They did. Her changes worked perfectly. Martha indulged in daydreams about the praise she would receive to the point of even hoping some of her old customers would recognize her hand in this.

At their next lunch, Martha couldn't help herself and giddily shared what she had done with Cindy. Instead of congratulating her industry, Cindy shifted uneasily in her chair, avoiding eye contact throughout the meal.

The following week, on a clear and sunny Tuesday morning, Martha's Vice President, Craig, summoned her to his office. She had spoken barely a dozen times to him previously, and rarely more than a basic hello.

Craig closed the door and ordered Martha to undo her changes immediately and re-generate form letters for those sent out already. When she asked him to reconsider, he shook his head. When she asked why, Craig mumbled something about company policy and client notification and other boss talk. When she asked if it was due to customer complaints, he glared at her.

"Just make the changes. If you refuse, I'll replace you with someone who will."

This remark, for some reason, made Martha want to laugh. She was reminded of the moment she received the news from the magazine, how she was stunned, scared, bitter, and not in control. Who was that woman? Where had she gone?

"You find this amusing?" Craig said. "You don't think we'll find someone who can do it, is that it?"

"No, that's not it at all," she said, even though she knew he couldn't find anyone else. He knew it as well as she did and at that moment that seemed the most important thing in the world to her.

"Well?" he said.

"I'll come in on the weekend and reverse the changes."

"I don't want to wait for the weekend," he said. "I want it fixed as soon as possible."

"As you wish."

Martha exited Craig's office in good spirits but then saw Cindy Palestro sitting in a chair as if waiting, leafing through a magazine. When Cindy looked up, she looked older, sadder, and clearly uncomfortable at the encounter. Martha winked at her friend that it was all okay.

GOING FORWARD

Josh's was the type of bar you went to without remembering why or how you ever came to do so in the first place. Just east of the downtown core, on a narrow side street in an industrial area, our weekly refuge from the office was a perfect antidote for five days of corporate dullness.

Dimly lit, as such places tend to be, there was an oppressive odour of beer, smoke, and a plethora of greases—worker grease, kitchen grease, motorcycle grease, and maybe some traces of elbow grease—seeping from the heavy, uneven wooden tables and chairs, and walls and ceilings. Knife scratches grooved in the over-varnished oak tables displayed many symbols and words, but no sentimental hearts or initials of lovers. The toilets, accessed by a steep descent along creaky stairs and then down a long, dark hallway of peeling wallpaper and slick condom ads, could lay claim to being the most disgusting in the city, a reputation its owner apparently cared little to change. Most importantly, Josh's beer was cold and cheap.

And boy was I thirsty. I ignored Raji and Charlie, who were sitting with the erstwhile Chester, and grabbed one of two near full pitchers of golden liquid.

"'. . . the new process will ensure optimum efficiencies,'" Raji was saying. "Going forward."

I almost spilled the beer while pouring.

"Easy," Charlie said.

But I was unable to contain my laughter at Raji's superb imitation of our director, particularly the way he captured Dean's deep pompous boom.

"Going forward?" Chester said. "I don't get that."

A fixture at Josh's long before we knew the place existed, Chester—we didn't know his last name—was short and thin with curly brown hair, the type who picked fights because of his lack of size.

One evening, after we'd been coming here for only a month or two, he asked to join us, as a tentative explorer might have done with natives, a full jug of beer his chest of trinkets. Ignoring our bemused looks, he began filling our glasses. Chester filled his mug last, lifted it up, and then swallowed the beer in one pull. Then he topped his up and sat down with us, and has ever since. We never minded because he continued to buy us pitchers and rarely disrupted our end-of-week unwinding. It must have made an odd first image to non-regulars, Chester in blue jeans and lumber jacket and the three of us with our freshly shaved faces and coordinated Dockers and golf shirts.

"So tell me, what does it mean?" Chester said, obstinately, after none of us acknowledged him.

"It's a euphemism," I said.

Apparently, Chester didn't know what that meant either. By the rapid rubbing of his chin between thumb and index finger, not to mention the seething glare from behind those thick brows, I could tell he was frustrated. A few years ago, such gestures would have signalled the onset of a fight, as we'd witnessed once.

"It's not a euphemism, just an expression," Charlie said.

"What does it express then?" I said, suddenly annoyed for some reason.

"Another way of saying, from now on," Charlie said.

"Precisely," I said.

"So what's your problem, Ben?" Charlie said.

"Boys, boys," Raji said, tapping the table with the bottom of his glass. "It doesn't mean a single thing whatsoever. It's an expression but one that expresses nothing. You take it out of any sentence, nothing changes. It's just extra verbiage, verbal litter, if you will."

The simplicity of Raji's interpretation seemed to satisfy Chester and Charlie, but not me. I should have let it go but damn it, I was still riled up from the last-minute meeting that had made me late. "Fellows, it's intended to sound like nothing precisely to hide the fact that it actually means something, something pernicious."

"Pernicious?" Chester said, as Raji and Charlie sighed and shook their heads slowly.

"Pernicious, yes, harmful, dangerous."

"Aren't you getting a little melodramatic there, Ben?" Charlie said.

He was probably right.

"Think about it guys," I said. "If you say, from now on, it implies something went wrong and someone is likely to pay for what happened. To say, going forward, on the other hand, is a way of saying that everything that was screwed up before gets swept under the rug, as long as we promise to play by the new rules in the future."

"And don't bring up the past," Raji said, nodding.

"Bingo," I said. "The past is assumed forgiven and forgotten. All the unpleasantness and problems vanish. Nothing to complain about, no one to blame, and so let's congratulate ourselves and go for lunch."

"Not, what have I done lately, but what can I promise not to do in the future," Raji said.

"A managerial pardon, for guys like Dean," Charlie said, thoughtfully, before letting out a burst of laughter.

"Not only that," I added, "the manager—Dean in this case—can leave the impression that it's a consensus rather than a decision."

"I don't see that," Charlie said.

"Me neither," Raji said.

"Think about it," I said, affecting more certainty than I felt.

Then I distributed the rest of the pitchers amongst the four glasses. I hesitated to look at Chester because by now, I expected him to be fuming, or ready to leave us and sulk at the bar. Instead, his eyes widened in a look of wonder, like a child's at his first zoo visit.

"You can do all that. With just two words?"

"Well, Chester, we can't, but our managers can," Charlie said.

When Charlie said that, the true impact of Dean's announcement revealed itself to us: we had a ton of work ahead of us. Not only to adapt to the new procedure, but also to fix up the previous mess. We drank our beers in silence, each hoping another would switch the topic. Meanwhile, something was brewing inside Chester's odd little mind, judging by his darting, lively eyes.

"Why can't I do that?" he said, all of a sudden. "I'm my own boss."

"Do what?" Charlie said.

"Go forward."

Chester's eyes grew wider, his mouth forming a strange half-smile, at once sinister and optimistic. He finished his beer, and walked out the door, without saying goodbye. Not even to Jen, who was approaching our table.

"Hey, do you think he'll come back?" Raji said, picking up the empty pitcher.

"Why?" I said.

"Well, he's only covered one pitcher on his tab," Raji said.

Jen smirked and then turned her back to Raji and looked at me, rolling her eyes. I smiled. "Jen, another please, on our tab."

A week of spiriting sunshine concluded with grey skies and a constant November drizzle the following Friday. The change in weather felt less ominous, though, than Chester's absence. Without him, we were once again self-conscious in Josh's, as if our legitimacy in the place came only via Chester. This was silly because no one was paying us any particular attention.

"You guys are drinking slow today," Jen said, pointing at the pitcher, still one-third full.

"Where's Chester?" I said.

"No idea. I haven't seen him since he was with you guys last week. I think Josh is worried about him."

"Worried about Chester, or his most lucrative regular?"

Jen frowned and glared at Raji. Then she emptied the pitcher into our glasses, and waved the empty jug at the three of us.

"And how long do you plan to nurse the next one?"

"Touché," Raji said.

His slight blush and weak smile disarmed her and made me wonder if there was something going on between the two of them. In her early thirties, Jen was only a few years older than we were and she had a nice body, with a smooth, flat belly teasingly exposed by a short, torso-hugging t-shirt. Her nose, which may have been broken at one time and not properly reset, made her face homely at first but more appealing after each jug. And Raji was no Adonis himself. He could have benefited from losing a few pounds and gaining a pair of contact lenses.

"What do you know about the guy?" I said, to Jen.

"Me? You're the ones who spend so much time with him."

That was true but we knew nothing about him, not even his last name. Whenever we asked Chester about his personal life, he'd change the subject, usually by pointing to one of the half dozen television screens surrounding us and coming up with some trivial sports statistic or anecdote. We didn't know if he had family, parents, wife, children, nor even where he'd been born. His age was a mystery too and he could have been anywhere between his late twenties and early forties. I wasn't sure Chester was even his real name.

"Actually, outside of sports, he doesn't talk much," I said.

"When he does, who can understand him?" Charlie said.

"Whatever," Jen said.

"What about Josh?" I said. "What does he—?"

"There he is," Raji said, pointing to the entrance.

I had to look twice because I almost didn't recognize Chester. Our beer benefactor was a different man, his stature taller, his smile wider, and his stride less hesitant than I'd ever seen. He'd shaved. In a way, he looked almost too alive and too normal. The lumber jacket was gone, as were the faded jeans, replaced by a windbreaker over a long-sleeve shirt and—I couldn't believe my eyes—a pair of pressed beige gabardine pants. I feared he was about to try and sell us Bibles.

"Chivas neat, and make it a double, please," Chester said, to Jen.

She gazed at Chester as if waiting for the punch line to a distasteful joke. When none came, she huffed and gave him a look she might give to a child who needed scolding.

"You know I can't do that, Chester," Jen said.

His face became blank, as if he didn't even know who she was, let alone what her words meant. But instead of protesting, he went to the jukebox. Jen glanced at us for support but we were just as bewildered by his sudden forgetfulness.

One night, perhaps a few weeks after we'd started coming to Josh's, but before he began joining us, Chester provoked a fight with a customer. That customer turned out to be Josh's cousin. No one knew about the familial connection at the time and, for some reason, Josh was not there that day. Several regulars got involved—not us, we weren't regulars yet so we stayed far back—all supporting Chester. The cousin had brought a few friends with him too. Punches connected and bottles broke; barstools and chairs crashed. By the time the police came, it was a full-scale brawl, just like in the movies. No one was seriously hurt, though, and no one was arrested.

Josh had to have been intimidated by the army Chester had summoned not to banish him from the bar. The cousin never showed his face again. Chester apologized, paid for the damages, and then blamed his inability to handle hard liquor for his part in the fight. A dubious but convenient explanation. Chester vowed to stick to beer from then on and Josh officially restricted him from ordering spirits. How Chester could have forgotten this all of a sudden was a mystery.

Chester returned from the jukebox, his face transformed, peaceful, as if he'd experienced an epiphany.

"Of course, I'm sure Josh has his reasons. May I have a clean beer glass then?"

Jen seemed shaken by the exchange, almost paralyzed. She jumped when the piercing opening note of "Dreamer" by Supertramp came on. I emptied the rest of the pitcher into Charlie's glass and followed her to the bar where she was leaning over. When Josh, a young guy like us but better looking and built like a linebacker, finally looked up, she pointed to our table.

"I saw him come in," Josh said. "I'm glad he's back."

"I'm not so sure. He just tried to order a double Chivas."

"Is that so?"

"I talked him out of it but, get this, he didn't seem to understand why."

"That is strange. Another pitcher, Ben?"

"Yes, please."

"What's eerie is how calm and happy he looks," Jen said. "I bet you could give him that Scotch with no trouble."

"Oh?" Josh said.

"And another glass," I said.

Josh pointed to a plastic tray corralling a load of clean glasses. I freed one for Chester and one for me. Josh had finished pouring the pitcher then, so I took that too, leaving Jen and her boss to resolve what, if anything, to do about Chester's Scotch request.

Back at the table, Charlie and our enigmatic friend were in an earnest discussion that seemed to be frustrating both of them. Raji touched my arm as I sat down and then drew me close.

"Ben, I think Chester's lost it," he whispered.

"What do you mean?"

"You say one thing to him and he responds clearly but if you say another he's clueless. There's no pattern I can figure. I wonder if his mind's going, or his memory, or both. How old do you have to be before you can get Alzheimers?"

I tried to follow what Charlie and Chester were saying. It was like watching a dubbed foreign film where the soundtrack was off a couple of beats. They appeared to be talking about hockey, with Charlie griping about the Leafs and their latest losing streak and Chester—the biggest Leafs critic we knew—contrarily optimistic about their future. Their alternating smiles of comprehension followed by quizzical looks of confusion made the conversation dizzying. Like a rollercoaster, with alternating dips and climbs of sense and nonsense.

"So how've you been Chester?" I interrupted.

He turned to me. His face was blank and I feared he didn't recognize me. Raji gave me an I-told-you-so elbow nudge and then nodded to urge me on. I glanced at Charlie who just shrugged. The Supertramp song finished and Blue Oyster Cult's, "Don't Fear the Reaper," started. Chester smiled and shook my hand.

"Hello Ben. Enjoying your beer, I hope?"

"So what've you been up to?" I said. "You haven't been around Josh's much lately, I hear."

Chester reacted as if I was speaking another language. I glanced at Raji and Charlie again. They looked bored, having suffered through this phase already. Meanwhile, Chester said nothing. Did he understand my question? Maybe he thought it was rhetorical.

"Everything okay, Chester?"

"Sure, just a few guys having a few beers."

The simplest statement said with the most profound yet calm conviction that nothing else matters in the entire world, or rather, that there was nothing else in the world.

"Cheers," Raji said, raising his glass.

The clinking of our glasses echoed his sentiment. Although I wasn't satisfied with this brief chat, I was glad to have disentangled from it.

The three of us began discussing the latest reorganization rumours. Chester listened with such unusual intensity that I felt like a specimen in some kind of scientific experiment. Clearly, he couldn't follow the names and details. Yet his scrutiny didn't waver until we began talking nostalgically about people we'd worked for in the past. At a pause, like an impudent and impatient child, he declared that the Cincinnati Bengals would win on Sunday at Mile High.

Raji, a diehard Broncos fan, couldn't ignore this. "The Bengals! Over Denver? That's crazy."

"The Bengals haven't even won as many games as the Broncos have lost," Charlie said.

Chester ignored Charlie and looked at Raji. "I don't think it's crazy."

"Care to make it interesting?" Raji said.

It would be a dumb bet. Especially for Chester, whose encyclopaedic sports knowledge and gambling prowess constantly impressed us. Not only could he predict whether teams could cover the spread, he often predicted spreads before Vegas published them. But now Chester acted as if he truly believed the Bengals would not only cover the thirteen points, but also win the game outright. He raised two fingers. Raji nodded, raising two fingers of his own, and then they shook hands to formalize the wager.

Chester finished his beer and said goodbye, without looking back, just as Styx beckoned us to "Come Sail Away".

"What was that about?" Charlie said, after our gambling expert was gone.

"So unlike him to make that kind of a bet," I said.

"Maybe he's got some inside info," Charlie said.

"It would take a hell of a lot of unreported injuries to change that outcome," I said.

"Maybe the game is fixed," Charlie said.

"You know, now I feel bad for taking his bet," Raji said.

"He can afford it," Charlie said.

Then together we realized Chester's absence meant we'd have to cover the entire bill again, including Chester's drinks. The others bellyached about this but I was glad to return the favour for once, although also relieved Josh had banned him from those expensive Scotches.

Raji had no difficulty overcoming his guilt after Denver's 35 - 3 win. He was in high spirits at work all week, impatiently biding his time until Friday when he would collect. At Josh's, we found Chester waiting for us, along with two full pitchers and four glasses.

"Have a seat, guys," Chester said, and started pouring. "These are on me, an early Christmas present."

We exchanged glances but had no response other than to accept and drink. I could see Raji itching to bring up the bet and his restraint impressed me. After a toast to the future, Chester reached into his pockets, pulled out two crumpled one hundred dollar bills, flattened them on the table, and pushed them to Raji.

"Here, for you," Chester said.

Raji meekly thanked him, any desire to gloat neutralized by Chester's uncharacteristic calmness. As generous as Chester was sharing his money, when it came to gambling, he was a sore loser. He'd moan for weeks over bad bets, which occurred rarely. And this had been about as bad a bet as I'd ever seen him, or anyone, make. But now Chester seemed cheerful about it, acting as if it wasn't even his money, that he was only the messenger.

"Thanks, but I feel I took advantage of you," Raji said.

This confused Chester, and so I asked him if he remembered why he had to give Raji the money. Our friend became visibly perplexed and annoyed before turning his head up at the televisions. I repeated my question.

"I just know I have to give it to him, I owe it to him."

"Do you even remember the bet?" I said.

It was like talking to a simpleton. Then he pursed his lips, like an obstinate child refusing to go to bed.

"I do not remember. I know."

"Chester, where were you yesterday?" I said. He gave me the blank stare I expected. "All right, Chester, what are you doing tomorrow?"

"The zoo, if the weather's good," he said, his boyish smile inducing an involuntary smile of my own.

But my smile faded quickly. Somehow, I knew his beer buying days had passed because, in Chester's altered mind, they had never happened.

At least that was my theory. I said nothing about this to Raji and Charlie, letting them cling to the faint hope the old Chester, the one who used to buy pitcher after pitcher, the one who seemed to need our company, would return.

The following Friday, Chester's mood once again was jovial. I sat down at our table but he remained standing.

"Fellows, I only have time to share a single pitcher. But I'm buying."

"What's your rush, Chester?" Charlie asked.

He shrugged, adding a goofy smile as if to say he had no idea.

"So, go do what you have to do and come back," Raji said.

"I always go forward. I never come back."

Chester continued smiling after he said this but something in his smile had changed. After he left us, we sat silent for a couple of minutes. Another pitcher arrived. Courtesy of Chester, Jen told us. Charlie poured, and Raji raised his glass in salute.

"That guy is a complete mystery. But I'll drink his beer anytime."

"Oh, guess what you missed from Dean at today's meeting?" Charlie said, addressing me in particular.

"Just spit it out," I said.

"He changed the process again, contradicting the previous one."

"So now we are back to doing exactly what we did before," Raji said. "So then, are we going backward now? Because we were going forward. Or are we going forward now, because we were going backward?"

Charlie nodded vigorously before twisting his face to mimic Dean's, and clearing his throat.

"'Whether forward or backward, at the end of the day—'"

"Hey guys," I said, "what say next week we check out some other bar? Just for a change, you know."

THE I. T. DIRECTOR

I. THE KINDS OF SYSTEMS AND HOW THEY ARE ACQUIRED

In business organizations, processes exist that are either manual and performed directly by humans, or automated as part of computer systems managed by Information Technology (IT) departments.

Computer systems are either established, with a support structure in place, or they are new. New systems may be newly developed or new only to an IT director, inherited through an organizational change or merger. IT personnel who develop, support, and maintain computer systems may be accustomed to reporting to a director or they may operate autonomously.

Computer systems may be assigned to a director by others, or he may acquire them externally, as with a purchased software package, or develop them with his own abilities and resources.

II. OPERATIONAL SYSTEMS

This discussion will be limited to processes automated by computer systems and will describe, in the order given above, how such systems are obtained by a director, and how they are to be managed and sustained.

Established systems where the director and his team know each other are easier to manage than new ones. The director just needs to avoid innovation and not upset habitual methods and procedures evolved by his predecessors, modifying them only for changes in circumstances. This way he can simply monitor problems as they arise. It should be easy for a director of average ability to maintain his position in all but the most extraordinary situations.

III. NEW SYSTEMS ADDED TO EXISTING ONES

It is more complicated with new systems. First of all, if the system is operational, but appended to a director's portfolio, problems arise from an inherent expectation that the experienced director will bring about improvement. This is a delusion because things can only deteriorate before they improve. The acquiring director is obligated to impose his own methods, as well as present to senior management a cynical assessment of what he has inherited to justify the resources needed to better the situation. This results in resentment from those who were against the change, and an inability to meet the expectations of those who put the director there because one cannot force them to accept this truth nor to support its demands. And a director cannot push too hard out of the greater necessity to maintain goodwill.

New systems will either come from within the same organization or not. It is easier to control and secure those that do, as it is enough to neutralize the influence of the previous director, which may only require restraining individuals loyal to him. Aside from that, the familiar environment ought to ensure a smooth transition. While some adjustments to procedures may be necessary, the incoming employees should easily integrate with existing staff. The new director who wishes to control this new system and its staff has only to bear in mind two considerations. The first is to remove or reassign the direct reports of the former director, and the second is not to alter the job titles, geographic location, or pay of the current staff. Doing so ensures integration with the existing team does not take long.

Systems acquired from external organizations in other geographic locations require great effort, combined with good luck, to control. Physical relocation by the new director gives the best chance of success, as it will entrench his position. Being close, he detects problems and issues as they spring up, and can quickly fix them. From a distance, one only hears of problems and issues when they become serious, when it is too late. Also, proximity inhibits anyone trying to take advantage of a director's unfamiliarity with this system for his own purposes. Furthermore, employees are happy to have direct access to their director and, if they choose to cooperate, are more inclined to respect him. If they desire to be adversarial, his presence will make them fear him.

A more practical approach is to exchange current staff with persons holding key positions in the new system. Unless this is done, or the director does not put himself physically there, he will need to assign a manager.

The cost of exchange can be contained within an existing budget, and the risk of upset to people minimized, as it only affects the ones whose work and responsibility are taken away. And with less responsibility, those people have little power to cause problems. Those not affected will be careful not to make mistakes, afraid that what happened to their peers could happen to them. In short, an exchange costs little because one can count on one's own people to be more honest. Fewer problems arise and anyone who feels wronged due to their diminished capacity can cause little trouble.

It should be noted that an employee either ought to be treated well or the opposite. They are likely to avenge small upsets but not large ones. Therefore, if one is to take actions that adversely affect people, one ought to act in such a way as not to be concerned about resentment.

If the director chooses to add a manager, he assumes an incremental cost. The acquired system ends up affecting the director's operational budget, creating further problems when these costs ripple through and affect other obligations, such as training, travel, raises, bonuses, and so forth. In order to cover this additional expense, he will be compelled to lean on everyone, which affects morale. Therefore, adding new management is as useless as exchanging staff is useful.

When acquiring a new system, the director should try to gain control of as much as he can, including peripheral systems, centralized staff functions such as business analysis, support, architecture, data management, and project management, as well as any ongoing projects affecting these systems. These he should stop or slow down. He should also strive to weaken the influence of powerful stakeholders, taking care that no peer should, by accident or implication, assume responsibility for what now belongs to him.

Organizational changes always introduce a level of discontent or restlessness either through an excess of ambition or through fear. What happens is that as soon as a capable director takes control, those with little power are drawn to him, motivated by envy of whoever held power over them previously. The director does not have to try hard to win them over, as they will align with him immediately. Yet he must be mindful that they not get too comfortable and gain leverage. He must ensure that with his own strength and with their support he keeps complete control. A director who is not vigilant on these points will quickly lose what he has gained and, while doing so, encounter endless misery.

The wish to increase one's extent of control is natural and commendable for directors and they do so when the opportunity arises and, when successful, they earn regard and perhaps promotion, not criticism. But when they lack the ability or means, but still try, then they deserve the bad results that come to them.

One rule rarely fails: he who is the cause of another's rise in the organization will himself experience a downfall. This is because the promotion has been brought about either by astuteness, or else by will, both traits distrusted by the director who has risen.

IV. MERGERS AND RE-ORGANIZATIONS

Considering the difficulty of controlling newly acquired systems, it is interesting to examine what occurs when it happens on a large scale. For instance, when two companies merge or there is a major shuffling of responsibilities across an IT department.

A director manages systems in two ways: either he manages them closely with powerless subordinate supervisors, or he delegates control to managers. Such empowered delegates recruit their own people who come to recognize this manager as their leader and hold him in natural regard. In systems managed closely by a director, his employees have higher regard for the director because he is the superior and, if they do report to a supervisor, it is for administrative purposes only, without any particular affection or loyalty. When large-scale changes such as mergers occur, it is easier to deal with the systems that were controlled with the director having the power, because then there is only one person who needs to be eliminated or persuaded to the new director's side. With divided powers, this takes more time, and the effort becomes wearisome.

V. HOW TO CONTROL SYSTEMS WHICH WERE AUTONOMOUS

There are three ways to acquire systems previously managed autonomously, that is without a formal reporting structure, under control. The first is to assimilate that system's functions within one or more of the director's existing systems, the next is to manage those systems directly, and the third is to permit them to continue working under their previous practices, adapting the team structure in such a way to ensure they follow direction. Once this adapted structure realizes it cannot survive without the director's support, they will work hard and remain loyal. If they feel confident their group is not threatened then this is the easiest way to manage it.

Where another director previously managed the system, with a staff conditioned to his management style, the employees lack the ability for self-management and so are less resistant to the introduction of a new director. He can win them over more easily. But if they were autonomous before, they developed energy and spirit, which can foster resentment and a rebellious attitude that will never permit them to forget their previous independence. In this case, the safest approach is to neutralize this energy through absorption, or manage them closely.

VI. NEW SYSTEMS DEVELOPED THROUGH ONE'S OWN ABILITY

The purest scenario occurs when someone rises to become director by developing and implementing new systems of significant size. This offers an opportunity for advancement, one based on accomplishment and excellence.

With newly developed systems, the difficulty in managing the system and its staff will be determined more or less according to ability. That he has risen to such a level of responsibility to lead a large development in the first place implies either ability or good luck. So it goes that one of these two factors will mitigate difficulties. The aspiring director who relies least on luck is the strongest.

Those who become directors relying on their own ability and resources develop and implement their systems with difficulty, but manage them with ease. During development, challenges arise in part from the methods and procedures they use to establish authority and control. There is nothing more difficult, more risky to one's reputation, and more uncertain of success than to lead change, whether with IT staff in managing the development or those on the client side who will receive the system. New systems are countered by those who have prospered from the previous methods, and complacent participation from those who, although they could benefit from the newly automated procedures, are ignorant of that possibility. This partly comes from their reverence for those who argue for tradition, but also arises from man's basic fear of change. Therefore, whenever those who resist change have a chance, they will fight, while the others offer meek support, causing corresponding grief.

To be thorough, it is necessary to consider whether a director should acquire power and use it to advance his aims or whether he can rely on persuasion. With the latter, they succeed badly and never accomplish anything, but when they have power and use it forcefully to resolve an issue, they will rarely encounter trouble.

All directors who have power succeed, and those who rely on the trust and goodwill of others fail. Aside from this, the nature of people is variable and while persuasion is easy to effect, it is difficult to sustain. Therefore, a director must take such measures that, when people stop cooperating, it is possible to compel them.

VII. PACKAGES OR NEW SYSTEMS DEVELOPED BY OTHERS

Directors who do not develop and implement systems themselves, who rely on purchased packages, customized or not, have little trouble acquiring systems but much trouble managing them. By avoiding the difficulties of development, they nevertheless encounter them when the system is in operation. These are directors whose systems are built by others and whose success, regardless of the diligence applied in selection, depends on chance and on the abilities of those who have done the work for them, two inconstant and unstable things.

Software packages are intended to meet the needs of a wide variety of clients, possibly for multiple industries. Thus, out of necessity, they are simplistic and, excepting core business functions, a poor fit for the particular needs of the purchaser. The situation worsens when the package is customized to adapt to existing business processes and interfacing systems for this work cannot be done without the package vendor. The changes, usually rushed and based on fluctuating needs and variable interpretations of how an organization functions, create an unstable compromise. They spoil the purity of the original package and key elements such as documentation and training, and the new software inevitably falls short of what was promised. The director ends up with a system he does not understand well enough to manage with strength.

Directors with such systems, like everything in nature whose growth is contrived, lack strong roots and foundations and therefore crumble as soon as they encounter trouble. This is unavoidable except when they possess such abilities to discover a way to lay the foundations after the fact.

VIII. THOSE WHO BECOME DIRECTORS THROUGH OTHER MEANS

Two methods of acquiring systems outside of chance and ability ought to be mentioned. These are when, through deceit, a director acquires control of systems, or when a system sprouts up independently of IT, from within a functional business organization, elevating one from that area to a position of influence in IT.

Examples of deceit include misrepresentation of personal experience and abilities, taking credit for the efforts of others, and political manoeuvring. Of these methods, some may wonder how such individuals can remain secure in their position unchallenged. It depends on whether they have used their tactics badly or properly. Those that can be called properly used, if they can be spoken of respectfully, are those that are essential to that particular situation, applied with one stroke, and then dropped when no longer needed. The badly employed are the ones that start slowly but escalate with time. In these cases, it is impossible for the director to survive indefinitely.

A director who takes such routes should examine all the tactics necessary and execute them so as not to have to use them again. Then he can still win people over. Otherwise, he will forever have to be willing and prepared to act in this way.

Above all, a director must manage his employees and handle his dealings in a consistent way so that whatever happens, favourable or otherwise, he does not vary his conduct. For when things turn sour, it is too late for harsh tactics and, in good times, his generosity will seem disingenuous and will not be rewarded with appreciation.

IX. CLIENT DEVELOPED APPLICATIONS

There is the increasingly common situation in which a business unit, shunning or shunned by an IT department, automates internal processes using consumer software development tools. Expedient patchwork solutions such as these often morph into the size and complexity of a system, but one that is maintained within the business unit. Such systems, created without a long-term strategy, let alone a formal development methodology, may be called client-developed applications.

It inevitably comes about that the business unit will ask the IT department to take over such applications. But this demand always comes with the condition there are no changes to its accessibility, flexibility, and low cost of operation. On the other hand, the IT department, largely because of that ungovernable accessibility and flexibility, will want to stabilize the application or, more likely, replace it, usually at significant cost. These contradictory stands will bring about one of three results: a robust and supportable system, no change, or disaster.

An IT director inheriting a client-developed application experiences new complications because he must deal with end-users who have become ersatz IT developers. Worse, these developers are lulled by frequent successes into believing their accomplishment is as good as, if not superior to, anything IT could have produced. An IT director cannot control these user-developers to his liking, whereas his corresponding business director has their allegiance. The IT director should try to win over the user-developers, which he can do easily if he transfers them to his staff, and makes them part of his team. For when people are treated well by those from whom they expected bad treatment, they will be bound more closely. Thus, being technically inclined, they become more quickly devoted to the IT director than to their former superior outside IT. The ways to win their allegiance are numerous and vary according to circumstances. The important point is to ensure the dealings remain friendly, as there is no security in acrimony.

Even so, such applications are liable to encounter danger when they come under the control of the IT director for they will be managed either directly or left in charge of the newly transferred user-developer(s). In the latter case, control is weakened because it rests entirely on the goodwill of a user-developer who, in times of adversity, can damage the director with great ease due to the volatility of the system. They can do so either overtly or through defiance. The director, in such situations, is unable to exercise absolute authority because the ultimate loyalty of the transferred individual remains with those for whom he built the system in the first place. When things are quiet, they are acquiescent and promise their support, but in troubled times, when truly needed, the director finds them recalcitrant.

X. HOW THE STRENGTH OF EVERY DIRECTOR CAN BE MEASURED

An important point to consider when examining the characteristics of a director is whether he has enough resources so that, when the need arises, he can manage his obligations independently or whether he must rely on the assistance of others. Directors who can handle unforeseen circumstances as they arise with their own resources are strong. Those who have only enough resources to cover planned work and require outside help when unforeseen problems or opportunities occur are weak. For weak directors, one can say little, other than to encourage them to pay attention only to important areas and allow others, when necessary, to be neglected.

XI. EXTERNALLY MANAGED SYSTEMS

Still to be discussed are outsourced systems, those operated by external organizations that remove the responsibility of staff management from the director. Once implemented, they can be managed with little ability for the responsibility lies outside the organization, and these systems will remain stable regardless of how the director acts. He is detached in such a way that these systems alone are completely secure from his organization's point of view.

This distinction makes it pointless to discuss them further. Nevertheless, the circumstances behind a vendor attaining such a level of influence and trust are worth exploring.

Common to all organizations is the notion that senior management gives more credence to external parties, such as vendors and independent consultants, than they do to their own people. Sales staff of vendors exploit this prejudice, proposing solutions comparable to what the organization can produce on their own, but cheaper and quicker, often combined with software packages as discussed above. IT directors cannot match these claims without misrepresentation or committing their staff to a large burden. From his perspective, the IT director may be won over by an opportunity to save himself much effort. However, once entrenched, the vendor cannot be removed without extreme effort.

XII. THE KINDS OF RESOURCES, AND CONCERNING CONTRACTORS

Having covered the various types of systems, the means of acquiring, managing, and retaining them, and, to some degree, the causes of their success or failure, what remains for discussion is the people who build and support them.

By now, the importance of a director laying his foundations ought to be clear; otherwise, it follows, failure is certain. The basic pillars of the management of computer systems, whether new, old, or a combination, are good methodologies and good resources. Since good processes cannot exist without the power to enforce them, it stands to reason that where there is strength, there will be good methodology and so a discussion on internal processes performed by IT resources can yield to one on the nature of the resources themselves.

The people under the control of a director report directly to him or are hired under contract, independently or through agencies, or they come from other parts of the organization, possibly resource pools.

Borrowed staff of any kind, whether from pools or contracted, are useless and dangerous. If one uses independent contractors to develop systems, the systems they develop will never be stable or reliable. For contractors are disunited, disruptive to staff, opportunistic, lack discipline, and their methods and results are proprietary. They speak well and are confident while things run smoothly, but in times of turmoil, they become defensive and act meekly and timidly. They have no fear of reprisal nor are they obligated to be loyal to anyone. Failure is only avoided as long as problems are. They feel no motivation to perform beyond ensuring future revenue. Indeed, it is often in their best interest to produce poor results to increase an unwitting director's dependency on them.

To take it further, contractors put in a leadership position are either capable or they are not. If they are, one cannot trust them because they always aspire to their own greatness and nurture dependencies. If they are not capable, then it is obvious what their impact will be.

XIII. VENDORS, RESOURCE POOLS AND DEDICATED STAFF

Contracting staff from vendors is a tempting option when one is in need of a quantity of people to respond to an unplanned situation. These people may be useful and competent individually but, for the director who calls on them, they are always disadvantageous. When they fail, the director is exposed. When they succeed, he incurs a dependency, as the work done by vendor staff is, consciously or unconsciously, proprietary because it is performed using the vendor's methods, standards, and procedures. Therefore, a director will continually need the vendor to maintain what they developed. Any director looking to fail should resort to this type of resource, which is far more dangerous than the use of independent contractors. People who work for vendors are united and wholly loyal to someone else, whereas independent contractors take longer to instil themselves. Independent contractors take direction from someone the director appoints and therefore do not have the authority to develop a dependency quickly.

The wise director always avoids either of these resources and develops his own, willing to fail with them rather than succeed with others, acknowledging that true success is unachievable with outside aid. In practice, though, when directors spot a quick fix possibility, they become blind to these dangers. Therefore, if a director cannot recognize the negative impacts of his choices until they arrive then he is truly unwise. Sadly, such insight is rare.

A variation of this is the centralized pooling of resources by function or skill sets within an IT organization. These resources are available to directors for a limited but sometimes protracted period. Due to organizational constraints or regulations, a director may have no choice but to resort to this type of resource, which, while not as risky as borrowed staff from outside, still poses problems. That they work for another means the director must ensure good relations with his colleague, remaining constantly in debt. Worse, the director cannot control all the employee's work assignments, nor can he control performance appraisals and remuneration, and therefore may end up with someone who not only has mixed loyalties, but also mixed responsibilities.

No system is secure without its own dedicated resources and, conversely, without them it becomes entirely dependent on chance. Nothing is as uncertain or unstable as authority not founded on its own strength. One's own resources are those hired by the IT director, those who report to that director, and those whose performance ranking and pay fall under the control of that director.

XIV. HOW A DIRECTOR SHOULD ORGANIZE HIS STAFF

A director should have no other aim or thought than to improve his systems, their management, and the processes used to control them. For the art of managing computer systems is his primary function. Directors will surely fail when they exploit the benefits of the position and the first cause of losing his position is to neglect key leadership skills. What enables him to keep his position is the mastery of those skills, skills that can be passed on to those who follow him.

The inept director quickly loses respect and is despised, one of the primary criticisms a director should consciously guard against, as will be shown later. No comparison can exist between one who understands his systems and one who does not. Therefore, it is unreasonable to expect that those who possess such understanding should listen to, or obey, those who do not. From one there is disdain and from the other there is necessarily suspicion, so it is not possible for them to work well together. Employees cannot respect a director who does not understand his systems and his resources and how to manage them nor, conversely, can such a director trust and rely on them.

Directors should monitor the organizational climate closely, observe what is going on, and identify trends, taking advantage of slow and quiet periods when he has opportunity to do so. Knowing his organization, he is better able to protect his interests and is better prepared for change. If it becomes necessary, he can abstract from this knowledge and apply it to other organizations similar to his.

A wise director studies those he respects, how they behave in various situations, examining the causes of their successes and failures, so as to avoid the latter and imitate the former. He should never succumb to complacency in stable times, but should use those periods to fortify his position and organize his resources with diligence, in order to prepare for any adversity or exploit any opportunity that comes his way.

XV. THINGS FOR WHICH DIRECTORS ARE ADMIRED OR FAULTED

Aside from measurable performance factors, how a director should act towards his staff, clients, and peers, along with how he should do so in a direct, useful manner by dispensing with deceptions such as political correctness, ought to be discussed. For how someone behaves in real life is so far removed from what should be done that anyone who neglects reality for what appears morally correct will soon enough cause his own downfall. Anyone who wishes to live up to an artificially haughty level of virtue quickly encounters the true nature of people. Therefore, it is necessary for a director wishing to succeed to know how to do wrong, and then make use of that knowledge, or not, according to necessity.

All people, especially directors for being centrally placed, gain reputations for qualities that can be faulted or admired. So it is that one director is reputed generous, another stingy. One is deemed encouraging, one critical; one harsh, one kind; one deceitful, another honest; one weak and vacillating, another confident and decisive; one polite, one arrogant; one open and trusting, another paranoid; one sincere, one duplicitous; one stubborn, another wavering; one confrontational, another compliant; one bureaucratic, another efficient; one task-oriented and concise, the other sociable, and on and on.

Naturally, it would be preferable for a director to exhibit all the above qualities generally considered as good, but this is not practical. Human nature does not permit it and the division of labour within bureaucratic organizations, such as IT departments, particularly those with matrix organization structures, makes it inadvisable. The director must distinguish how to avoid the consequences of the negative traits that would hurt his reputation, and how to refrain from those that could destroy him. If his character makes certain traits impossible, he should not concern himself so much about the latter. Also, he should not worry about the results of characteristics without which his position cannot easily be maintained. To sum it up, something that appears a virtue, if followed, will be a director's undoing, while another trait that seems negative, when followed, brings security and success.

XVI. GENEROSITY AND STINGINESS

In the first pair of above named traits, it would be considered positive for a director to be known for being generous with his resources. However, if exercised in a way that he does not gain credit for it, generosity harms the director, for if one goes about it honestly, as should be done, it may go without notice, and then the director still cannot avoid the discredit of its opposite. Therefore, no one wishing to gain a reputation of generosity can afford to miss any future opportunity to bolster that reputation. This type of director will have his reputation central in all his acts and eventually will be compelled to burden his staff to maintain it. Then he will lose support and be of no value to anyone. With his generosity having put off many, for little profit, he becomes vulnerable to any minor setback and the first real trouble will bring him grief. When he realizes what is happening, and then reacts, he will necessarily gain a negative reputation for being stingy.

Since a director cannot consciously gain from pleasing everyone and earn credit for it, at least not without great cost, he should not fear a reputation of stinginess. In time, he will gain more repute for this than for being generous. Through the economical use of his resources, he will be prepared when troubles arise, and he can still engage projects and respond to unforeseen problems without burdening his staff. In the end, he actually proves generous to those he does not burden, who are the majority, and stingy toward those he does not oblige, who are few.

There may be examples of directors who have reached their positions by never declining requests. One either is established as a director or is rising to that position. In the first case this is dangerous but in the second it is recommended. Where directors have had success being generous with their resources, they either used their own or those of others. With his own, he should be sparing, but with others, he should neglect any temptation to avail himself. For the rising director, going forth to acquire systems and obtain resources from others, this willingness to take on work and responsibility is necessary; otherwise, no one will support him.

Nothing wastes as rapidly as generosity and eventually one runs out of resources and the means to accommodate or, in avoiding that, one burdens one's staff to the point where they hate their director. Above all, a director should guard against spite and hatred and a generous nature leads to both. Therefore, it is wiser to have a reputation for stinginess, which brings reproach without hatred, than to seek a reputation for generosity, reproach being preferable to hatred.

XVII. HARSHNESS AND KINDNESS, LOVE AND FEAR

As for the other qualities mentioned above, every director should desire to be considered kind and not harsh. Nevertheless, he should take care not to misuse this kindness. A director, so long as he keeps his staff united and loyal, should not mind a reputation of harshness because, with a few examples, he will appear kinder than those who, through too much gentleness, allow problems to fester. These problems affect all under him whereas his censures are to the individual only.

Of all directors, it is impossible for the new director to avoid harshness, owing to the difficulties encountered with newly acquired systems. Still, he ought to be slow to act on assumptions, refrain from showing uncertainty, and proceed in a deliberate manner, applying wisdom and understanding. He must ensure that overconfidence does not make him hasty before too much distrust makes it impossible for others to tolerate him.

This raises the question of whether it is better to be liked than feared or feared than liked. It could be said that the answer is a blend of the two but, since it is difficult to achieve and maintain a precise mix in one person, it is safer to be feared than liked. Generally, a director's superiors, peers, and staff can be considered ungrateful, self-absorbed, untrustworthy, cowardly and greedy, but as long as they are treated well, and there is success, they can be counted on. But when things turn badly, they will turn against the director. Whoever relies entirely on goodwill and neglects other precautions is lost. Friendships gained through favours and not ability may indeed be genuine, but they are not secure, and in times of difficulty become unreliable. People worry less about offending one they loved than one they feared. As the friendship exists only through obligation, owing to the fickleness of people, it is broken at every opportunity. But fear preserves a director, due to an aversion to discipline, and this deterrent still works.

A director ought to instil fear in such a way that, if he cannot win their esteem, he avoids their hatred. He can endure very well being feared while he is not hated, which works as long as he avoids overburdening his staff. In cases when he must encroach on them, he needs good cause, and the ability to justify it. Above all, he must keep relationships impersonal because people forget heavy burdens more quickly than they do insults. With a large team then, it is quite necessary for the director to disregard the reputation of being harsh, for without it, he would never hold his staff united or obligated to its duties.

Again, on the question of being feared or liked, people grant amity according to their own will, and fear according to that of the director. A wise director should establish himself on what is in his own control and not that which is in the control of others; he must strive only to avoid hatred, as has been repeatedly stated.

XVIII. HOW DIRECTORS SHOULD HONOUR THEIR WORD

Everyone would acknowledge how admirable it is for a director to honour his word and act with integrity, not cunning. Nevertheless, experience shows that successful directors put little stock in being completely honest and forthright. They understand how to deal with people ambiguously and therefore, in the end, surpass those who stand on principles.

One can direct with integrity or by deceit and intrigue. Because the first is frequently not sufficient, it is often necessary to turn to the second. The director must know how to make use of both approaches. When the need for intrigue is evident, it is necessary to know well how to disguise it, and to be a good actor and dissembler. As people are simple, self-absorbed, and fully attendant to their immediate needs, he who seeks to deceive will always find someone willing to be deceived.

It is unnecessary for a director to have all the good qualities mentioned so far, but it is very necessary to appear to have them. And to this should be added that to have them and always observe them is harmful, and that to appear to have them is useful. To appear considerate, honest, confident, trusting, upright, and to be so, but to have a mind ready so that should one require it, one knows how to change to the opposite. A director, especially a new one, cannot observe all those things for which men are admired, often being forced, in order to maintain or improve his position, to act contrary to those ideals. His mind must be ready to turn itself accordingly, as circumstances dictate.

For this reason, a director should take care to never let anything slip that is not replete with those positive qualities, that he appears to anyone who sees him as altogether considerate, honest, confident, upright and trusting.

Everyone sees what one appears to be, few really know what one is, and those few dare not contradict what the majority see. People are judged by results. For that reason, let a director have the credit for being able to develop and maintain his systems, as the means will always be considered honest. Everyone will admire him because what a thing seems to be, combined with positive results, universally impresses. The few who know the facts will have difficulty finding an audience.

XIX. THAT ONE SHOULD AVOID BEING HATED

The characteristics mentioned above are the important ones, but there are others that should be covered, keeping in mind the point made all along that a director must consider how to avoid what will make him hated, or contemptible.

It makes him most hated to burden his staff, in support of his own ambitions, to the point it impinges on personal lives, a temptation from which a director must abstain. When peoples' lives are left to be and respected, the majority will work contentedly and submissively. The director only has to concern himself with the ambition of a few, whom he can curb with ease in many ways.

A director becomes contemptible when considered fussy, superficial, weak, and indecisive, all traits from which a director should guard himself as if they were actual enemies. And he should try to show in his actions greatness, fearlessness, gravity and resolution. In his private dealings with his staff, he should show that his decisions are fixed and final so that no one can hope either to deceive him or circumvent him.

The director who can cultivate this reputation will be highly regarded and he who is highly regarded will not be easily countered. Provided it is known that he is competent and esteemed by his staff, he can only be challenged with difficulty. For this reason, a director should have two fears. One from within, on account of his staff, and the other from without, on account of external powers and ambitions. From the latter, strong resources and good relations with his peers, inside and outside the IT department, protects him.

With his staff, when external troubles arise, he only has to fear conspiracy, from which a director can easily protect himself by keeping his people satisfied with him and avoiding being hated and despised. Anyone interested in challenging his control expects to please everyone by the director's removal, but when the outcome can only upset people, adversaries will lack the confidence to try.

For this reason, directors should not worry about conspiracies when his people hold him in esteem, but when they are hostile and bear hatred, he should fear everything and everyone. Wise directors, those with well-ordered teams, will have taken every precaution not to incite extreme reactions from senior management and to keep their employees satisfied and contented, one of the most important goals of a director.

With so many interactions with people of varying levels, directors cannot help being hated by someone. So they should avoid being hated by every one, and when they cannot manage this, they should endeavour, with the utmost diligence, to avoid the hatred of the more powerful. It should be noted that hatred can result as much from good actions as bad ones. Therefore, as stated before, a director wishing to maintain his position is often forced to take actions generally not considered positive. For when the people one relies on act in a manner that is negative, one is compelled to act in like manner. In those situations, good actions will actually do harm.

XX. IF CERTAIN TACTICS OFTEN USED BY DIRECTORS HELP OR HURT

To hold their positions securely, some directors have rescinded authority from their staff, divided their teams into factions, fabricated challenges to overcome, and worked to win over those they distrusted in the beginning. Some have demanded their approval be sought on every matter while others have delegated responsibility. Although one cannot judge these things without proper context, each can be addressed generally.

A new director never rescinds authority from his staff. Instead, if he finds them without any, he always gives them some. By doing so, he brings them to his side, and those he has misgivings about become loyal. Those already loyal will not only remain so, but will also give their devotion. Naturally, not everyone can be given authority, but when it is given to some, one can deal more confidently with the rest, as a title increases the obligations of those given authority. The rest grasp this distinction when they connect the responsibilities of that prestige with favourable treatment.

When a director takes away authority, he causes offence by showing distrust. Even if justified, such a move breeds contempt. Because one cannot manage everything oneself, it follows that a director must turn to contractors or other external help, the consequences of which have already been discussed.

A new director with a new system always allocates authority to his own people. However, when a director adds a new system to an existing portfolio, it is necessary to remove the authority of the incumbent staff, except for anyone who assisted the director in its acquisition. But even these people should have their powers weakened over time to the point where the director is comfortable with all his leaders.

Dividing teams into factions and promoting conflict and competition between them may be a tempting way to divert staff from upward ambitions. But it is not a useful approach because it always results in an imbalance of weakness and strength within the team. It becomes easier for those with strength and with designs on a director's position to succeed, as the weak will certainly join them. This exposes vulnerability in the director because such factions would never be tolerated in a strongly directed team.

Without a doubt, directors develop strong reputations when seen overcoming difficulties and obstacles. Recognizing this may motivate a cunning director to fabricate challenges so that, once having successfully resolved them, his reputation grows. A new director with a new system can benefit more from this tactic than an established one.

It is common for directors, especially new ones, to find more help from those whom in the beginning they distrusted than those who were trusted. This is not certain and depends on variable factors but, in general, those who at the beginning were hostile, who now have few alternatives remaining, can be won over with the greatest ease. They see it is necessary, through their actions, to improve the original impression the director formed of them. Thus, the director gets more out of them than from those who have worked for him longer and have become complacent.

When a director acquires a new system with political help, he ought to understand the motivation behind that aid. If it is not a natural regard but fuelled instead by discontent, then he will keep his supporter's goodwill with great difficulty, for it will be impossible to satisfy him. Given human nature, it is easier for the director to make friends of those who were content with the previous management, and therefore not originally on his side, than with those who favoured him because they were unhappy with the previous situation.

A director, in order to hold his position more securely, may intervene as the sole authority with all external groups and demand direct involvement in all decisions. Micromanagement can be a useful tactic, or not, according to the particular circumstances, and can help in one way but harm in another. If the director finds it more difficult to control his own people than those from outside then he ought to adopt this approach. If he has more to fear from external influences then he is better off to delegate and spread the responsibility.

The best security is to avoid being hated because, no matter what bureaucratic measures are put in place, they will not protect a director who is hated. The hatred will inspire discovery of ways to circumvent those measures.

XXI. HOW A DIRECTOR CAN GAIN REPUTE

Nothing builds a director's reputation more than great accomplishments and setting a fine example of personal qualities. It is profitable for a director to give clear demonstrations of his capabilities by developing strong systems and maintaining or increasing their strength. It also behoves him to give shining examples of his ability to manage and control people along with keeping their loyalty. Above all, a director must strive to win a reputation for outstanding ability.

No director should think he can choose perfectly safe courses. Instead, he should expect to have to take risky ones because it comes about that, in avoiding one trouble, he will run into another. Wisdom comes from knowing how to distinguish the characteristics of troubles.

A director should promote ability in his team by honouring and giving credit to great achievements. At the same time, he should encourage his staff always to act professionally and calmly, both internally and with those outside the group. His staff should be willing to take risks and actions to further their own positions, without fear that credit will be taken from them. Furthermore, he should periodically engage in and support social activities that can maintain or increase the morale of his staff. But he must ensure his participation is done in a dignified manner for he cannot let anything mar his image.

XXII. THE DIRECTOR'S MANAGEMENT TEAM

The choice of managers, supervisors, and other leaders is crucial to a director and he can be judged based on his selectiveness. The first opinion one forms of a director comes from observing the people he has around him. When they are capable and honest, the director may be considered wise, because he knows how to recognize the capable, and how to keep them loyal. But when they are incompetent, one cannot form a good opinion of the director, for he made a fundamental error in choosing them.

To enable a director to assess manager or supervisors under him, there is one test that never fails. Regardless of ability and technical proficiency, a manager who attends to personal ambitions beyond those of the director's, will never make a good aide, nor will the director be able to trust him. He who is entrusted with the affairs of another should never think of himself, but always of his superior, and never pay attention to matters that do not concern the director and his systems.

From his standpoint, the director should be considerate to his managers and supervisors, trust them, pay and reward them suitably, and share with them both credit and responsibility. This will allow them to see that they are dependent on the director and, benefiting from it and being entrusted with so much responsibility, they will desire no more and only fear changes, not initiate them. When relations are managed this way, there is trust, but when it is otherwise, it will lead to disaster for either the director or the manager.

XXIII. HOW SUGAR-COATERS OUGHT TO BE AVOIDED

One danger to which directors are especially vulnerable, unless they are very careful and discriminating, is that of sugar-coaters or those people who are eager to please and who put a positive spin on everything to avoid conflict. Not sophists out for their own devious aims, nor sycophants currying favour, but rather people who wilfully, albeit often with good and unselfish intentions, frame what they say to diminish the pain of reality. The only way to guard oneself against this type is to let it be known that candidness will be tolerated. On the other hand, if such a policy is fostered universally, one loses respect.

A director compromises by selecting key people in his organization, giving only them the liberty of speaking the truth, and then only of those things about which the director asks. And he should ask and question them on every detail and fully listen to their opinions and then, afterwards, form his own conclusions. With these counsellors, separately and collectively, the director should carry himself in such a way that each of them knows that the more freely they speak, the more he will respect their opinions. Outside of these people, he should listen to no one, and then make and implement all decisions straight away, and be steadfast in his resolutions. He who does otherwise either becomes undone by the sugar-coaters, or ends up so diverted by varying opinions that he falls into contempt.

Taking counsel is essential for a director, but only on his terms and not when others wish. He should discourage all advice unless he requests it. But he should be a constant inquirer and a patient listener about the specific things he inquired. On learning that someone has not told him the truth, he must demonstrate his anger, clearly and openly.

Anyone who says that a director who is reputed for wisdom, is not wise from his own ability, but from the good advisers he has around him, are either deceived or trying to deceive. An innately unwise director will never take good advice, unless by chance he left it to an individual who happens to be wise. In this case, though, his position would be in jeopardy to that adviser. If an inexperienced director takes counsel from various sources, he will never receive a consistent picture, nor will he know how to integrate the information. Each source will think of his own interests and the director will not know how to interpret them. There are no exceptions because people will always prove untrue unless they are compelled to be honest. Therefore, it must be inferred that good counsels, no matter their origin, are borne of the wisdom of the director, and not the reverse.

XXIV. WHY DIRECTORS IN THE PAST HAVE LOST THEIR POSITIONS

The actions of a new director receive greater scrutiny than those of established ones. The above guidelines, carefully observed, will make a new director appear experienced and allow him to feel secure in his position, as if he had executed the role for a long time. When seen as capable, directors receive more loyalty and respect than what simple experience would bring, because people are more interested in the present than the past. When the present is fine, they look no further and they will support the director vigorously, as long as he does not fail them in other things. It could be a double victory to him to develop a new system, and then invest it with good procedures and good people, but it could also prove a double disgrace to him who inherits his position only to lose it due to a lack of wisdom.

If one considers directors who have lost their positions in the past, one finds that either their employees were hostile or, if they were friendly, the director did not know how to control his superiors. In the absence of these two defects, directors with enough resources cannot lose their standing.

Bad luck and bad timing are not good excuses for a director to explain a loss of position after many years, but it is rather their own inattentiveness to these things. In quiet times, they felt secure that nothing would change and afterwards, when things turned against them, they thought only of warding off the immediate difficulty, fighting symptoms instead of root causes, counting on their people to back them up. This course, when others fail, may succeed, but it is bad to have neglected all other factors, since one would never wish to fail depending on someone else. Only those who depend on the director, and his ability are reliable, certain, and durable.

XXV. DESTINY IN CORPORATE AFFAIRS

Some might argue that corporate affairs are outside of an individual director's control, that they are guided by the whims of senior management, or the economy, or world politics, or God. They subsequently might argue it is not necessary for a director to make an effort in immediate affairs, but rather leave them to destiny.

It is true that a director can be happy one day and ruined the next without his character or disposition having changed. From everything stated above, a director who relies on goodwill is lost when it leaves him. He who directs his actions in the spirit of the times will succeed just as he whose actions are not current with the environment will fail.

People use varying methods to achieve worthy goals such as respect, wealth, and happiness. One does so with caution, another with tenacity; one by force, another by skill; one by patience, another by its opposite; and each one succeeds in reaching their goals by a different method. Of two cautious men, one will achieve his goals and the other will fail. Similarly, two men will achieve the same goals but use different approaches, one circumspect, the other daring. All this is due to whether or not their approaches are suitable for the spirit of the times and political environment.

Whoever conducts himself cautiously and patiently, events being in accord with that method, will succeed. But if events change and he does not adapt his approach accordingly, then he will be ruined. It is rare to find someone shrewd enough to know how to modify his ways, because either he is unable to change his natural character, or he cannot talk himself into changing, and remains stuck using old methods that proved successful in the past. Therefore, the cautious man, when it is time to take risks, does not know how to do it and is ruined, but if he continually adapts his conduct to the times, his career will not be affected.

Nevertheless, in today's world of rampant complacency and feelings of entitlement, a director who exhibits the best values described above is destined to have a harder go of it than he might have at another time. On the other hand, anyone who has or develops the right skills can always rise above circumstances.

www.ingramcontent.com/pod-product-compliance
Lightning Source LLC
Chambersburg PA
CBHW071305130626
46556CB00003B/1475